CRICUT MAKER FOR BEGINNERS

QUICK & EASY GUIDE TO IMMEDIATELY START CREATING AND EARNING WITH YOUR OWN CUSTOMIZED PROJECTS WITH DESIGN SPACE

EMILY TYLER

© Copyright 2020 - All rights reserved.

The content contained within this book may not be reproduced, duplicated or transmitted without direct written permission from the author or the publisher.

Under no circumstances will any blame or legal responsibility be held against the publisher, or author, for any damages, reparation, or monetary loss due to the information contained within this book. Either directly or indirectly.

Legal Notice:

This book is copyright protected. This book is only for personal use. You cannot amend, distribute, sell, use, quote or paraphrase any part, or the content within this book, without the consent of the author or publisher.

Disclaimer Notice:

Please note the information contained within this document is for educational and entertainment purposes only. All effort has been executed to present accurate, up to date, and reliable, complete information. No warranties of any kind are declared or implied. Readers acknowledge that the author is not engaging in the rendering of legal, financial, medical or professional advice. The content within this book has been derived from various sources. Please consult a licensed professional before attempting any techniques outlined in this book.

By reading this document, the reader agrees that under no circumstances is the author responsible for any losses, direct or indirect, which are incurred as a result of the use of information contained within this document, including, but not limited to, errors, omissions, or inaccuracies.

TABLE OF CONTENTS

INTRODUCTION 6

CHAPTER 1: WHAT IS A CRICUT MACHINE AND HOW DOES IT WORK 12

- WHAT YOU CAN DO USING CRICUT 13
- CARTRIDGE 16
- MATERIALS THAT CAN BE USED WITH A CRICUT MACHINE 19

CHAPTER 2: SETTING UP YOUR CRICUT MAKER MACHINE 28

- SETTING UP THE MACHINE 28
- USING CRICUT SOFTWARE 29
- IMPUTING CARTRIDGES AND KEYPAD 30
- LOADING AND UNLOADING YOUR PAPER 31

CHAPTER 3: EVERYTHING YOU NEED TO KNOW ABOUT CRICUT DESIGN SPACE 34

- HOW TO DOWNLOAD CRICUT DESIGN SPACE 34
- CRICUT DESIGN SPACE TOP MENU 36
- HOW TO WELD 37
- HOW TO SLICE 38
- HOW TO FLATTEN 40
- HOW TO ATTACH 41
- HOW TO GROUP/UNGROUP 41
- HOW TO DUPLICATE/DELETE 43
- USING TEXT IN CRICUT DESIGN SPACE 43
- GETTING STARTED WITH TEXT 43
- HOW TO EDIT IMAGES IN CRICUT DESIGN SPACE USING THE SLICE TOOL 47

CHAPTER 4: SIMPLE PROJECTS TO START WITH 50

- CUSTOM GRAPHIC T-SHIRT 50
- STICKERS WITH YOUR CRICUT 54
- FALSE COWHIDE HOME KEYCHAIN 57
- CALFSKIN HAIR BOW 59
- SHAMROCK EARRINGS 62
- FUN FOAM STAMPS 64
- PERSONALIZED DOORMAT 66
- CRICUT BOOKMARKER 69
- PERSONALIZED PHONE CASE 72

CHAPTER 5: SPECIAL OCCASION PROJECTS 76
- CHIPBOARD TREE ORNAMENTS 76
- EASTER BASKET FUN 82
- VALENTINE'S GIFT TAGS 89
- HALLOWEEN T-SHIRT 91
- NO-SEW FELT NATIVITY FINGER PUPPETS 94

CHAPTER 6: HOW TO START SELLING YOUR PROJECT 96
- SELLING PRE-CUT CUSTOMIZED VINYL 97
- SELLING FINISHED PIECES 99
- PERSONALIZED CLOTHING AND ACCESSORIES 99
- MARKETING ON SOCIAL MEDIA 100
- TARGET LOCAL FARMER'S MARKET AND BOUTIQUES 101

CHAPTER 7: MAINTENANCE OF YOUR CRICUT MACHINE 104
- CUTTING BLADE 104
- SUBSCRIBE TO CRICUT ACCESS 105
- DE-TACK YOUR CUTTING MAT 106
- KEEP YOUR CUTTING MAT COVERS 106
- CUTTING MAT 106
- CLEANING THE CRICUT MACHINE 108

CHAPTER 8: COMPLEX OPERATIONS 112
- BLADE NAVIGATION AND CALIBRATION 112
- SET PAPER SIZE 114
- LOAD LAST 116
- PAPER SAVER 116
- SPEED DIAL 118
- PRESSURE DIAL 119
- CRICUT DESIGN SPACE 122
- CRICUT PENS 124

CONCLUSION 128

Introduction

Cricut Design Space is the online stage that Cricut designed to be utilized with their more up to date machines.

It's not programming – you download a module on your PC (or the application on your tablet/smartphone), and after that, you can design whatever you might want.

You can utilize designs and pictures that are now transferred into Design Space, or you can transfer your own!

Cricut Design Space is 100% free. You do need to make a record; however, if you would prefer not to, you don't need to spend a penny.

Cricut Design Space is an online programming program that enables you to interface with your cutting machines by means of USB or Bluetooth. It's the way you make the majority of the wonderful designs that will wind up on your tasks, shirts, cushions, espresso cups, and the sky's the limit from there!

As an option in contrast to making your own designs or getting them from Cricut, you can shop at Etsy (simply scan what you're searching for with SVG toward the end) and afterward "play with" designs.

While they have some free pictures and textual styles incorporated with the program, there are ones that you can pay cash for. You can likewise pursue a Cricut Access Plan, which will give you access to a great many pictures and textual styles. There are three pricing options: annual subscription for $95.88 per year, premium subscription for $119.88 per year and monthly subscription for $9.99 per month.

Be that as it may, you can introduce your own textual styles onto your PC and transfer pictures to Design Space (that you've made, found for nothing, or obtained without anyone else).

Cricut Design Space is an online program, so you don't download it onto your PC.

Nonetheless, you should download some modules, which should auto popup and brief you to download when you experience the underlying procedure.

If you are needing to download Cricut Design Space onto your iPhone or iPad, then you will simply need to go to the Apple App Store, scan for "Design Space," and it ought to be the primary alternative to spring up. Download it like you regularly would.

Any undertaking that you make in Design Space can be spared to the Cloud. You simply need to ensure you spare your venture – that catch is in the upper right-hand corner.

This enables you to see your task on any gadget where you are signed in.

Nonetheless, if you are dealing with an iPhone or an iPad, you have the choice to spare it just to your gadget. I would, for the most part, consistently propose sparing it to the Cloud, however!

You can utilize Design Space on Mac PCs, PC PCs, and iOS gadgets.

Your PC must run a Windows or Mac working framework, and hence, Google Chromebooks CANNOT be utilized, as they keep running on a Google OS.

Once in a while when you go to cut your design, it will stop you before you at the tangle see page and state you have to pay.

You may have incidentally included a picture that requires installment – you can return to your canvas and check each picture to check whether there is a dollar sign beside it (or check whether the text style you chose has a dollar sign. Remember that regardless of whether you have Cricut Access, you don't approach ALL the pictures and textual styles).

If you chose a venture from Design Space, it might have incorporated a picture or textual style that is paid. When you take a gander at the task guidelines, it should let you know if it is free or not.

I see this inquiry all the time in Design Space, and it very well may be so disappointing! Frequently, Design Space is down when they are making refreshes.

Some of the time, they will convey an email when they anticipate a blackout. However, I don't generally observe this.

If it's down, I would propose not reaching their client backing and simply be quiet.

You can likewise attempt another program or clear your program store, just to ensure it is anything but an issue on your end.

Cutting is one of my preferred highlights in Cricut Design Space! I cherish removing text styles and pictures in different designs.

Yet, now and then it won't work. If you are observing this to be an issue, here are a couple of thoughts:

- Make sure the picture/text style you are removing (so that is over another picture) is totally inside the other picture. If a bit of it is standing out, it won't cut.

- Make sure everything is chosen.

- Keep as a main priority that when you cut it, you will have two layers to expel from the picture – the first picture/text style that you cut, just as the cut

For what reason isn't Print and Cut working?

I won't jump a lot into Print and Cut, as it is a monster all alone.

Notwithstanding, the most compelling motivation why I see individuals experiencing difficulty with Print and Cut is that they didn't smooth their pictures! Before you go to print and cut, ensure you select all and press straighten.

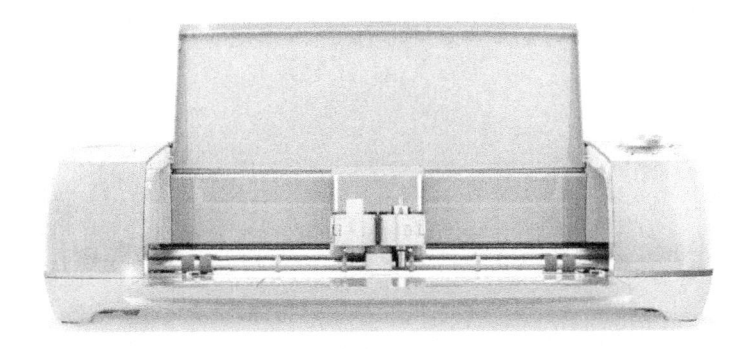

For what reason Can't I Open Cricut Design Space?

Regularly you will get a blunder or a white screen with Design Space if you don't have the most as of late refreshed module.

If you get a clear page, take a stab at invigorating the page to check whether the module update shows up. Try not to move far from this page when it's refreshing, or it will turn white.

CHAPTER 1:

What Is A Cricut Machine And How Does It Work

The Cricut is a cutting machine. This, at least, is the correct term. However, it does not in the least describe the infinite potential of this machine. I own the Cricut Maker, currently the best machine in the series. With the Cricut Maker you can do just about anything: cut different materials, custom t-shirts, sewing projects, postcards, birthday invitations, banners, creative lamps, stickers, bracelets, embossed creations, custom blackboards, mugs and glasses, cut out letters or images for scrapbooking, and much, much more.

What You Can Do Using Cricut

- Create stickers to stick in your car in your favorite items
- Create your own stencils for painting
- Create custom labels
- Personalize pillows, shirts, sweatshirts, tablecloths
- Produce an endless variety of Christmas ornaments
- Personalize glasses and mugs
- Engrave the plexiglass
- Make your own wall decals
- Create shapes from linden or balsa wood
- Create decals
- Making DIY slates
- Party banner
- Invitations for birthday
- Sewing projects
- Shapes for scrapbooking
- Leather items (diaries, bracelets, etc.)

- Puzzle

There are several different models, and the items that come with each machine vary from one to another. But there are some things that come universally with all machines.

Each machine comes with:

- A Cricut cutter
- One fine point blade and one premium blade cover
- A 12 × 12 inch "LightGrip" cutting mat.
- A USB cable
- A power adapter
- A welcome guide for easy setup
- A free trial membership for Cricut Access
- Access to 25 free projects ready to go
- Materials for a practice project.

Some models come with more elements, such as different blades, scoring wheels, or a special pen for writing.

The Cricut Machine is a plotter that can cut various materials and write / draw on them, it can also perforate them (create those tear lines typical of cinema tickets, so to speak), engrave them (for example Plexiglas and aluminum), create reliefs (such as in the case of embossing, even if in this house it is actually a debossing) or even folding lines (very useful if you make cards, tickets, boxes, etc.). The machine will do one or the other depending on the accessory (blade, tip or pen) that we are using. This machine is the Rolls Royce of cutting machines. And for good reason! Imagine any media up to 3mm thick, the machine will cut it with ten times the power of the Cricut Explore and its other competitors. What made me fall for this machine is the possibility of cutting leather. The Cricut machine can cut cardboard, balsa, vinyl, flex, burlap (!)... And FABRIC. Yes! You read that right fabric! And not just cotton! Not all kinds of fabric imaginable! In the Design Space you can find all kinds of fabrics: velvet, jersey, silk, lace! In all, the Maker cuts around 100 different materials up to 3mm thick. Another important feature of the Maker: you can write with it! Whatever the type of material we want to work with the maker (paper, wood, jeans ...), we will have to introduce it in the machine after making it adhere on special reusable mats , mats that are equipped with a more or less resistant layer of glue : if we are using paper we will use a mat with a layer of not very resistant glue, if instead we are using wood we will use a mat with a much more powerful layer of glue. The Cricut machine has a double carriage allowing two operations to be carried out in a single pass. It is thus possible to draw (or use the "scoring tool "to make folds) and cut at the same time.

Cartridge

Designs are produced using parts put away on cartridges. Every cartridge accompanies a console overlay and guidance booklet. The plastic console overlay demonstrates key determinations for that cartridge as it were. Anyway as of late Provo Craft has discharged an "All-inclusive Overlay" that is perfect with all cartridges discharged after August 1, 2013. The motivation behind the all-inclusive overlay is to simplify the way toward slicing by just learning one console overlay as opposed to learning the overlay for every individual cartridge. Designs can be removed on a PC with the Cricut Design Studio programming, on a USB associated Gypsy machine, or can be legitimately inputted on the Cricut machine utilizing the console overlay. There are two kinds of cartridges shape and textual style. Every cartridge has an assortment of imaginative highlights which can take into consideration several different cuts from only one cartridge. There are as of now more than 275 cartridges that are accessible (independently from the machine), containing textual styles and shapes, with new ones included monthly. All cartridges work just with Cricut programming, must be enrolled to a solitary client for use and can't be sold or given away. A cartridge obtained for a suspended machine is probably going to wind up futile at the point the machine is ended. Cricut maintains whatever authority is needed to suspend support for certain renditions of their product whenever, which can make a few cartridges quickly out of date.

The Cricut Craft Room programming empowers clients to join pictures from different cartridges, consolidate pictures, and stretch/turn pictures; it doesn't take into account the formation of discretionary designs. It additionally empowers the client to see the pictures shown on-screen before starting the cutting procedure, so the final product can be seen in advance. Referring to Adobe's surrender of Flash, Cricut declared it would close Cricut Craft Room on 15 July 2018. Clients of "heritage" machines were offered a markdown to refresh models good with Cricut Design Space. Starting on 16 July 2018, Design Space is the main programming accessible to make projects. Design Space isn't perfect with cartridges once in the past bought for the Cricut Mini, which was power nightfall in October 2018.

Third-party

Provo Craft has been effectively unfriendly to the utilization of outsider programming programs that could empower Cricut proprietors to remove designs and to utilize the machine without relying upon its exclusive cartridges. In a similar audit of bite the dust cutting machines, survey site TopTenReviews identified being "restricted to cutting designs from a gathering of cartridges" as a noteworthy downside of the Cricut run; however, the audit noticed that it could be an inclination for some. Two projects which could once in the past be utilized to make and after that get Cricut machines to remove subjective designs (utilizing, for instance, self-assertive TrueType text styles or SVG group illustrations) were

Make-the-Cut (MTC) and Craft Edge's Sure Cuts A Lot (SCAL). In April 2010 Provo Craft opened a lawful activity against the distributors of Make-the-Cut, and in January 2011 it sued Craft Edge to stop the conveyance of the SCALE program. In the two cases, the distributors settled with Provo Craft and expelled support for Cricut from their items. The projects keep on being usable with other home cutters. As indicated by the content of its lawful grumbling against Craft Edge, "Provo Craft utilizes different strategies to encode and cloud the USB correspondences between Cricut DesignStudio [a design program provided with the hardware] and the Cricut e-shaper, so as to secure Provo Craft's restrictive programming and firmware, and to avoid endeavors to capture the cutting commands".

Provo Craft battled that so as to comprehend and imitate this darkened convention, Craft Edge had dismantled the DesignStudio program, in opposition to the provisions of its End User License Agreement, along these lines (the organization affirmed) breaking copyright law. Provo Craft additionally affirmed that Craft Edge were damaging its trademark in "Cricut" by saying that its product could work with Cricut machines. Provo Craft declared this was likely "to cause perplexity, misstep or double dealing with regards to the source or starting point of Defendant's merchandise or benefits, and [was] prone to erroneously recommend a sponsorship, association, permit, or relationship of Defendant's products and ventures with Provo Craft."The consequence of this is clients with more seasoned variants of Cricut machines that were 'power dusk' by stopping of programming bolster have no elective programming to use with their now outdated machines.

Materials That Can Be Used With A Cricut Machine

There are many different materials that the machines can use for any project you desire, and we will be breaking down which machine can use what materials. Something that you should know is that there are materials that the maker can cut that the other machines cannot. Over one hundred different types of fabric as a matter of fact. The official website of the Cricut machines does change periodically in what they say the machines can cut and so you will need to check their website as a result of this. In doing so, you will realize what you can still cut and what may have been taken off of the list.

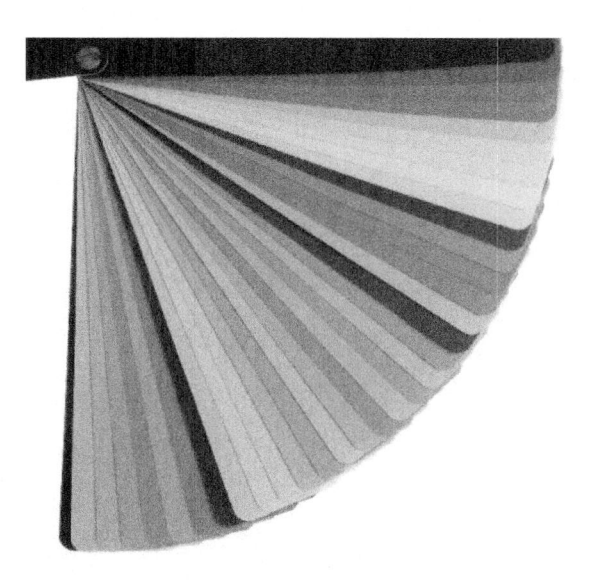

The explore series can only cut certain items and we are going to list them now.

The Explore series is able to cut these items:

- Tattoo paper
- Washi tape
- Paint chips
- Wax paper
- Faux suede
- Wrapping paper
- Washi paper
- Poster board
- Parchment paper
- Sticker paper
- Construction paper
- Photo paper
- Printable fabric
- Magnetic sheets

- Paper grocery bags
- Craft foam
- Window cling vinyl
- Cardstock
- Flannel
- Vellum
- Duck cloth
- Wool felt
- Cork board
- Tissue paper
- Duct tape
- Matte vinyl
- Iron-on vinyl
- Leather up to 2.0 mm thick
- Sheet duct tape
- Oil cloth
- Soda cans

- Stencil film
- Glitter foam
- Metallic vellum
- Burlap
- Transparency film
- Chipboard that is up to 2.0 mm thick
- Aluminum metal that is up to .14 mm thick
- Stencil vinyl
- Glitter vinyl
- Glossy vinyl
- Faux leather up to 1.0 mm thick

Fabrics, when used with the Explore series, need to be stabilized with Heat N Bond. Examples of fabrics are shown on the list below:

- Denim
- Felt
- Silk
- Polyester

Other items that the Explore Series can cut will be listed below:

- Chalkboard vinyl
- Adhesive vinyl
- Aluminum foil
- Cardboard
- Stencil film
- Dry erase vinyl
- Printable vinyl
- Outdoor vinyl
- Wood birch up to .5 mm thick
- Cardboard that is corrugated
- Shrink plastic
- Metallic vellum
- White core
- Rice paper
- Photo framing mat
- Pearl cardstock

- Cereal boxes
- Freezer paper
- Iron-on
- Printable iron-on
- Glitter iron-on
- Foil iron-on
- Foil embossed paper
- Neon iron-on
- Matte iron-on

The Maker can cut everything that the Explore series can cut but it can cut so much more because the Explore series operates with three blades but the Maker has six. The fact that they have the six blades, it is able to cut more fabric and thicker fabric as well. They also differ from the Explore series because the Maker doesn't have to use Heat N Bond to stabilize fabrics. This is a great thing because it means that you can go to a fabric store and choose a fabric and use it for a project with no preparation and no additional materials either.

The Maker is also able to utilize the rotary blade as well. This type of blade is new and it differs from the others that the Explore machines use because this blade spins and it also twists with a gliding and rolling motion. This rolling action is going to allow the Maker to cut side to side as well as up and down. Having a blade able to cut any direction is going to help you with the ability to craft great projects. The Maker is even able to cut (up to) three layers of light cotton at the same time. This is great for projects that need uniform cuts.

The Maker is also able to use the knife blade which is a more precise option and cuts better than the others before it. This blade can cut up to 2.4 mm thick. This machine is also able to use ten times more power to cut than the others as well.

With that being said, the Maker can cut over a hundred different fabrics that others can't. We will be supplying a list of some of those fabrics below:

- Waffle cloth
- Jacquard
- Gossamer
- Khaki
- Damask
- Faille
- Heather

- Lycra
- Mesh
- Calico
- Crepe paper
- Gauze
- Interlock knit
- Grocery bag
- Acetate
- Chantilly lace
- Boucle
- Corduroy
- EVA foam
- Tweed
- Tulle
- Moleskin
- Fleece
- Jersey

- Muslin
- Jute
- Terry cloth
- Velvet
- Knits
- Muslin

Remember that this is just scratching the surface of what the Maker can cut. There are many others because the Maker is considered to be the ultimate machine and the best of the four. The Maker is also great for sewing and there are hundreds of these projects on Design Space. Having a machine that is able to have access to these projects and the ability to cut thicker materials means that you have a machine that opens your crafting skills to a whole new level.

CHAPTER 2:

Setting Up Your Cricut Maker Machine

Setting Up the Machine

First, you'll want to set up the Cricut machine. To begin, create a space for it. A craft room is the best place for this, but if you're at a loss of where to put it, I suggest setting it up in a dining room if possible. Make sure you have an outlet nearby or a reliable extension cord.

Next, read the instructions. Often, you can jump right in and begin using the equipment, but with Cricut machines, it can be very tedious. The best thing to do is to read all the materials you get with your machine – while we'll go over the setup in this book, if you're still stumped, take a look at the manual. Make sure that you do have ample free space around the machine itself, because you will be loading mats in and out and you'll need that little bit of wiggle room.

The next thing to set up is, of course, the computer where the designs will be created. Make sure that whatever medium you're using has an internet connection, since you'll need to download the Cricut Design Space app. If it's a machine earlier than the Explore Air 2, it will need to be plugged in directly, but if it's a wireless machine like the Air 2, you can simply link this up to your computer, and from there, design what you need to design.

Now, once you have the Cricut initially set up, you'll want to learn how to use Design Space.

Using Cricut Software

So, Cricut machines use a program called Cricut Design Spaces, and you'll need to make sure that you have this downloaded and installed when you're ready. Download the app if you plan to use a smartphone or tablet, or if you're on the computer, go to http://design.cricut.com/setup to get the software. If it's not hooked up already, make sure you've got Bluetooth compatibility enabled on the device, or the cord plugged in. To turn on your machine, hold the power button. You'll then go to settings, where you should see your Cricut model in Bluetooth settings. Choose that, and from there, your device will ask you to put a Bluetooth passcode in. Just make this something generic and easy to remember.

Once that's done, you can now use Design Space.

When you're in the online mode, you'll see a lot of projects that you can use. For the purpose of this tutorial, I do suggest making sure that you choose an easy one, such as the "Enjoy Card" project you can get automatically.

So, you've got everything all linked up – let's move onto the first cut for this project.

Imputing Cartridges and Keypad

The first cut that you'll be doing does involve keypad input and cartridges, and these are usually done with the "Enjoy Card" project you get right away. So, once everything is set up, choose this project, and from there, you can use the tools and the accessories within the project.

You will need to set the smart dial before you get started making your projects. This is on the right side of the Explore Air 2, and it's basically the way you choose your materials. Turn the dial to whatever type of material you want, since this does help with ensuring you've got the right blade settings. There are even half settings for those in-between projects.

For example, let's say you have some light cardstock. You can choose that setting, or the adjacent half setting. Once this is chosen in Design Space, your machine will automatically adjust to the correct setting.

You can also choose the fast mode, which is in the "set, load, go" area on the screen, and you can then check the position of the box under the indicator for dial position. Then, press this and make your cut. However, fast mode is incredibly loud, so be careful.

Now, we've mentioned cartridges. While these usually aren't used in the Explore Air 2 machines anymore, they are helpful with beginner projects. To do this, once you have the Design Space software and everything is connected, go to the hamburger menu and you'll see an option called "ink cartridges." Press that Cricut, and from there, choose the Cricut device. The machine will then tell you to put your cartridge in. Do that, and once it's detected, it will tell you to link the cartridge.

Do remember, though, that once you link this, you can't use it with other machines – the one limit to these cartridges.

Once it's confirmed, you can go to images, and click the cartridges option to find the ones that you want to make. You can filter the cartridges to figure out what you need, and you can check out your images tab for any other cartridges that are purchased or uploaded.

You can get digital cartridges, which means you buy them online and choose the images directly from your available options. They aren't physical, so there is no linking required.

Loading and Unloading Your Paper

To load paper into a Cricut machine, you'll want to make sure that the paper is at least three inches by three inches. Otherwise, it won't cut very well. You should use regular paper for this.

Now, to make this work, you need to put the paper onto the cutting mat. You should have one of those, so take it right now and remove the attached film. Put a corner of the paper to the area where you are directed to align the paper corners. From there, push the paper directly onto the cutting mat for proper adherence. Once you do that, you just load it into the machine, following the arrows. You'll want to keep the paper firmly on the mat. Press the "load paper" key that you see as you do this. If it doesn't take for some reason, press the unload paper key, and try this again until it shows up.

Now, before you do any cutting for your design, you should always have a test cut in place. Some people don't do this, but it's incredibly helpful when learning how to use a Cricut. Otherwise, you won't get the pressure correct in some cases, so get in the habit of doing it for your pieces.

CHAPTER 3:

Everything You Need to Know About Cricut Design Space

How to Download Cricut Design Space

Visit design.cricut.com and you will be required to log in or create a username and password. Register your details on the website, and make sure you write down your login details, in case you log out in future.

Once you have taken care of that, click on a new project on the top right of the screen. This action will alert you to download the Design Space plugin. When the download process is complete, you will have to open the file, depending on your computer or browser.

If you are using a Chrome browser, it will on your download bar, located at the bottom. Click to open and click run or next, as prompted.

Follow all the download prompts. You will have to accept the terms and conditions and click install.

The procedure is straightforward, and the prompts will walk you through everything. Finally, Design Space is downloaded, and it's time to explore.

Before your machine can cut out projects, you will have to create your designs inside Design Space (also called Design Space canvas).

On the canvas, you will use the menu on the left side to kick off your designs.

- You will click upload to upload SVG files or images that you intend to cut. SVG is abbreviated for Scalable Vector Graphic and it is the most used file for cutting designs because it is explicit. SVG files can be found anywhere; you can find them on blogs, Etsy, and other places.

- The next menu on the left is Shapes. You can make use of stars, squares, circles, and other shapes to make your design. If you intend to scorecards or do other paper projects, you'll find score lines here.

- The third item on the left menu is text. There are a number of things you can do with text including; curving texts, making monograms, and using your personal fonts.

- The fourth item on the menu is Images. If you click the images icon, you will be redirected to the designs you can use if you are subscribed to Cricut Access or the designs you can buy from Cricut if you have no subscription.

- Fifth on the left menu is Projects. If you click on projects, you will see a display of projects that are up for sale. However, there is another dropdown menu that you can use to select your projects. Your saved projects are also located in that area.

- Sixth on the left menu is Templates. Some crafters do not use this feature, but you can use them to ascertain the size of the design you intend to cut and how it is meant to look on a shirt or apron. Mind you, it is used a guide, thus the actual template won't be cut out.

- Seventh on the left menu is the New+ button. If you want to start a new project, this is the menu to click. Always save your current project if you intend to keep it before starting a new one. The save button is located at the top right corner.

Cricut Design Space Top Menu

To understand Cricut Design Space, let's explore the top menu.

The top menu will only become available after you have texts typed out or a design uploaded. Thus, beginning from the left is the Undo button, used to rectify mistakes. The next button on the right is the Redo button, used to repeat and action.

The Deselect button is next, and it is used as the opposite of select. The Edit button is next and it has a dropdown menu that consists of copy or paste and flip. Next is the Size button; you can use it to change the actual size of your design or explore the bottom right of the design to use the two-way directional arrow.

Right at the bottom left of the canvas is the unlock button. This feature consists of a four-way directional arrow used to widen designs without making them taller or making them taller with making them wider.

Next on the menu is the rotation tool, used to rotate designs to every degree possible. The last feature on the top menu is the x and y coordinates, used to position designs on the canvas.

How to Weld

It can be a little bit daunting for a Cricut Space beginner to use the weld tool, however, when you become proficient, it'll open the doors to many more projects because it is a tool that will be used often.

The weld tool is located at the bottom right corner of Design Space, under the layers panel. Other tools close to it are; flatten, contour and slice tools.

In Cricut Design Space, the weld tool does the following;

- Connects cursive text and scrip in order for it to cut as a single word instead of individual letters
- Merge multiple layers and shapes into a single layered image
- Take of cut lines from different shapes and cut them as one big image

i. For you to use weld, the text or shapes you intend to weld together must be touching or overlapping each other.

ii. To select the layers you intend to weld together; select a layer, hold down 'ctrl' and select the other layer. After selecting both layers, click 'weld'. If you intend to weld the whole layers on your canvas, click 'select all' to select all the layers and click 'weld'.

iii. If you weld different layers together, it becomes a single image and will cut out in one color and on one mat.

Without selecting multiple layers, the weld option will not be available for use.

In order to weld texts, you have to make sure that the letters are all touching each other. Thus, you have to reduce the spacing of the letters until they begin to touch each other. Once you do this, you can select everything and click weld.

How to Slice

The slice tool is a feature in Cricut Design Space that cuts one design element out of another.

You can use it to cut text from a shape, cut one shape from another shape, or cut overlapping shapes from each other. Below is an example, and we will cut text out from a heart shape;

i. Choose a font

Use any font you prefer, but decrease your letter spacing from to 0.9 so that your letters will link together.

ii. Weld the text

When you're done with the spacing, you have to transform your letters into a single image by using the weld tool.

When you weld your letters, it permanently connects all the design elements into one image.

iii. Choose an SVG

You can find a heart SVG from Lovesvg.com.

You just need to ungroup everything and simply delete the unwanted elements.

iv. Set the size of your design

You need to resize the image.

Depending on the size you want, simply type the intended size on the width box.

For this example, we'll stick to 5.5 inches.

v. Arrange the design

You need to arrange the text and heart, by clicking 'arrange'.

vi.   Use the slice tool

When you have arranged your design perfectly, select your text and hold down 'ctrl' key, select the heart and click 'slice'. Now, you can remove the text from the heart and delete.

vii. Once your design is done, it is time to cut vinyl.

How To Flatten

The flatten tool is a feature used to turn multi-layered images into a single-layered image.

What Does Flatten Do In Cricut Design Space?

With the flatten tool, you can achieve the following;

- Remove cut lines from an image
- Transform multi-layered images into a single layered image
- Used to transfer regular images into printable images for print-and-cut
- Used to maintain distinct colors of multi-layered images

Using the flatten tool;

- To select the layers you intend to flatten together, lick 'select all' or hold down 'ctrl' and select the layers
- After selecting, click flatten at the bottom right corner
- When you do that, the image is now flattened.

How to Attach

Basically, there are two distinct reasons for using the attach tool;

- To keep scoring/writing lines in the right place
- To keep shapes in the correct place on the mat as on the canvas

Using the Attach tool to maintain the same arrangement

If you want all the pieces of your project to remain in the exact location during cutting, as it is on your CDS canvas, you have to;

- Select all the items of each color
- Click 'attach' at the lower right corner
- Repeat the process for each color layer until they are all nested under a label that says "attach'

With the attach tool, you will be able to cut out your projects exactly the way you arranged them on your Cricut canvas.

How to Group/Ungroup

Group on Cricut Design Space means to group two or more layers into one layer. On the other hand, Ungroup means breaking up a layer group into separate layers. There are different types of group layers, and if a layer is grouped multiple times, you will have to ungroup them multiple times, in order to completely separate them.

Group: To group, you have to select the layers you intend to group together by clicking your mouse and dragging on the design or select multiple layers in your layer panel by using a keyboard shortcut. To select multiple layers, you have to press 'ctrl' and select your layers on your computer. After selection, you have to right click your mouse and click the Group button. If you wish, there is also the option of creating multiple groups within groups, because it makes it easier to deal with complex designs.

In Design Space, groups work better with layers, especially when you're trying to manipulate some parts of a design. With Group, you can easily resize or stretch the selection.

Ungroup: It is very easy to ungroup designs that are grouped together.

To ungroup, you need to select the layer you intend to ungroup, right click your mouse, and click on the Ungroup button or select Ungroup. There are layers that might have been grouped multiple times, thus, if you intend to completely Ungroup, you have to continuously select again and again, and keep clicking Ungroup, until it's completely done.

The primary reason for using the Ungroup feature is to change or manipulate some part of a design. The change could be physical, or it could be manipulating some parts of a design by welding, attaching, or using some other methods, without touching on the rest of the design.

How To Duplicate/Delete

If you intend to duplicate a layer or set of layers, you have to select the part of the design or the layers you intend to duplicate, right click your mouse and click the Duplicate button.

On the other hand, if you intend to delete a single layer or a set of layers, you have to select the part of the design or the layers you intend to delete, right click your mouse, and select the Delete button.

If you have two designs and you intend to retain only one, select the design you intend to delete, right click your mouse, and click the Delete option.

Using Text in Cricut Design Space

Once you sign into Cricut Design Space, select one of the three places marked with arrows to start a new project. Then click the three line icon on the top left to proceed for a 'New Project'. As you start a new project, you will be directed to a gridded design space called a Canvas. Select the left sidebar which contains the text icon. A small box will emerge, shown by a second arrow, in which you can enter your text. Once the text entered, chose a font which can be found on the far left arrow.

Getting Started with Text

Start typing your text by simply clicking the text icon located on the left toolbar. A text box will appear in which you can start inserting your text. Font, style, and size as wells as line spacing and letter spacing can be selected by going on the top toolbar. It is advisable to type your text first and then make the changes you want afterward.

Fonts

The function 'Font' will display a diversity of fonts to choose from. You have the option to see only your fonts by clicking on system or to see those available by Cricut fonts by clicking on Cricut. If you have a preferred font in mind, then use the search option. Finally, you have the option to filter the fonts if you look for a writing or multilayer font.

How to Add Your Own Fonts

If you rather prefer to add your own Fonts, then sites are available such as CreativeMarket.com, TheHungryJpeg.com or DaFont.com which will offer a large selection to choose from. Also, DesignBundles.net provides creative bundles to buy with fonts and designs that have a commercial use license so you can resell them without any risk. Creating your own items to be sold requires that the Font comes with a commercial license. After having selected the Font you want to work with, find the file on your computer and open it. As Fonts come in a zip file, it is required to open the extract files which has been opened very likely automatically. Once the files extracted, variations of the Font will be displayed as 'Original', 'Italics' and 'Bold'. It is not necessary to install all the variations as often the 'Original' can easily be modified in your design software.

In addition, two versions called 'Open Type Font' and 'True Type Font' is offered. Their installation depends very much of the system you use. So, try both. Once the file you want is selected, right click on it and install. The new Font chosen will appear under 'System Fonts' in the Design Space. While in the process of installing a new Font, it is advisable to close design space and re-open it to see your new Font.

How to Access Special Characters

You can access special characters by using Humble Scrip which provides many options. You can access it by typing 'character map' in your system search box. The app will appear. A drop-down menu indicates which Font you are working with. Secure the option 'Advanced View' is properly checked. Then modify the Character set to Unicode and finally group by Unicode Subrange. At this stage, a new box will appear for the Unicode Subrange. Scroll it all the way to the bottom and select 'Private Use Characters'. In regards to your design place, if you wish to delete a letter from your text box and have it replaced, then hit control plus the 'V' key at the same time to paste your new special character. The configuration will look like a square but the text will change. If you wish to change the size, just use the Font size on the top toolbar. Once you are satisfied with the final result in terms of the sizing and spacing of your text, just highlight and select. Then click the align button on the top toolbar. If you wish, you can choose to align your text either to the left, or center it or align it to the right.

How to Curve Text

Curving text is rather simple to achieve in design space as it consists mainly to slide the text to the left.- By doing so, your text will curve up. Once this is done, you can use the letter spacing option if you need to make adjustments. Finally, you can select everything and center your lines.

How to Make a Stencil

Great for hand painted signs, stencils in design space can be created with the shapes tool on the left toolbar. By clicking on the unlock button situated on the bottom left, you can stretch your shape into a rectangle. Insert the text you want on your stencil, with or without the tips referred earlier in regards to centering, spacing, sizing, curvings or fonts. Once you are satisfied with the final result, then highlight and select all text and click the attach button on the bottom right toolbar. Select both the text and the box followed by selecting the align tool on the top toolbar.

How To Use Contour With Text

Contour is used to delete or hide unwanted pieces of a design or image. To use the contour tool, you have to select the image or layer (one at a time) you intend to edit and click on the contour tool located at the end of the layers panel.

By default, it is impossible to use the contour tool on text, and one of the reasons is that text is dependent on the font itself.

Thus, the program will reject any excessive modification involved with contour.

You have to weld your text before you can use the contour feature, and to do this, you will select the text or word you intend to use and click the weld button at bottom of the Layers panel. After welding, you'll be able to contour your texts or word and do away with the letters or blanks spaces that you intend to discard.

Remember to save a copy of your text if you intend to use it in the future, because after you weld it, you won't be able to edit it afterward.

How To Edit Images In Cricut Design Space Using The Slice Tool

You can use the Slice tool to edit images in Cricut Design Space. To do so, these are the following steps;

- Add your uploaded image to your canvas in Cricut Design Space. To do this, click on the image and click on insert images. The program allows users to upload more than one image at a time to the canvas.

- To work on your project, you have to expand the size of the image by clicking the right bottom corner and dragging it down a little. Do it until you can clearly see all the elements of the image.

- If there is any part of the image you intend to get rid of, you can use the slice tool to cut it off. On the left side toolbox, click on Shapes, then click on the square.

- Click on the left bottom circle under the square to unlock it. If you see a lock icon, click on it. When you do this, you've successfully unlocked the square, thus you can move it in any shape you want by using the right bottom circle. You can use the square to replace the deleted part of the image.

- With the square highlighted, press and hold the shift button. Click the bubble image with your mouse. This action highlights both of them.

- With both the image and square highlighted, use your mouse to click the slice tool at the bottom right corner.

- Pull away the pieces of your slice and delete if you want.

- Go on with the process until you successfully edit the image

-

CHAPTER 4:

Simple Projects To Start With

Custom Graphic T-shirt

Materials

- The Cricut machine
- Vinyl for the letters
- Your Cricut tools kit

Directions

Start by choosing the image you want to use. This can be done in Photoshop or you can place your text directly into the Design Space.

Next, open the Cricut Design Space. Choose the canvas that you wish to use by clicking the Canvas icon on the dashboard which is located on the left-hand side. Select the canvas that you will be using for your vinyl letters. This can be anything within the categories they offer.

Then, select the size of the shirt for the canvas. This is located on the righthand side of the options.

Now, click Upload for uploading your image, which is located on the left-hand side. Select the image you are using by browsing the list of images in your file library. Then, select the type of image that you have picked. For most projects, especially iron-on ones, you will select the Simple Cut option.

Click on the white space that you want to be removed by cutting out, remember to cut the insides of every letter.

Next, be super diligent and press Cut Image instead of Print first. You do not want to simply print the image, you cut it as well.

Place the image on your chosen canvas and adjust the sizing of the image.

Place your iron on the image with the vinyl side facing down on the mat and then turn the dial to the setting for iron on.

Next, you will want to click the Mirror Image setting for the image before hitting go.

Once you have cut the image, you should remove the excess vinyl from the edges around the lettering or image. Then use the tool for weeding out the inner pieces of the letters.

Now you will be placing the vinyl on the shirt.

And now, the fun part begins. You will get to iron the image on the shirt. Using the cotton setting, you will need to use the hottest setting that you can get your iron. There should not be any steam.

You want to warm the shirt by placing the iron on the shirt portion that will hold the image. This should be warmed up for 15 seconds.

Next, lay the vinyl out exactly where you want it to be placed. Place a pressing cloth over the top of the plastic. This will prevent the plastic on the shirt from melting.

Place your iron onto the pressing cloth for around 30 seconds. Flip the shirt and place the pressing cloth and iron on the back side of the vinyl.

Flip your shirt back over and begin to peel off the sticky part of the vinyl that you have been overlaying on the shirt. This will separate the vinyl from the plastic backing. This should be done while the plastic and vinyl are hot. If you are having trouble removing the vinyl from the plastic backing, then place the iron back on the part that is being difficult. Then proceed to pull up and it should come off nicely.

This should remove the plastic from the vinyl that is now on the shirt. Place the pressing cloth on top of the vinyl once again and heat it to ensure that the vinyl is good and stuck.

Although there are tons of steps, it is still an amazingly simple process.

Stickers with Your Cricut

Materials

- Cricut Explore Air 2
- Printable sticker paper by Cricut

Directions

Log in to your Cricut Design Space account.

In the Cricut Design Space, you will need to click on Starting a New Project. Then, select the image that you would love to use for your stickers. You can use the search bar on the right-hand side at the top to locate the image that you want to use.

Next, click on the image and click Insert Image so that the image is selected.

Click on each one of the files that are in the image file and click the button that says Flatten at the lower right section of the screen. This will turn the individual pieces into one whole piece. This prevents the cut file from being individual pieces for the image.

Now, you want to resize the image so that it is the size that you wish it to be. This can be any size within the recommended space for the size of the canvas.

If you want duplicates of the image for sticker sheets, you should select all and then edit the image and click Copy. This will allow you to copy the whole row that you have selected. Once you have copied, you can then edit and paste the multiple images to make a sheet. This is the easiest way to copy and paste the image over and over again.

At this time, you are ready to start printing your stickers. Click the Save button on the left-hand side of the screen to save the project and chose the option Save as Print and then Cut Image. Once done, you can click the green button that says Make It. This will be located on the section to the right of the screen.

Verify that everything is how it needs to be and click Continue. This will give you a prompt to print the image onto your paper. Make sure you have used the sticker paper for the stickers. Otherwise, it won't work.

Print out the image with your printer. If the Cricut sticker paper is too thick for your printer, using a thinner sticker paper is fine.

After the design is printed, adjust the Smart Set dial to the appropriate setting. Place the paper onto the cutting mat and load it into the Cricut machine by pushing against the rollers. Press your Load and Unload button that is flashing.

Press Go, and this will begin to cut your stickers. Since the stickers are small and intricate you will need to be patient.

A tip for getting a good cut is to not touch the mat and once the first cut is made and done, repress the flashing button to recut the stickers on the same lines that were previously cut.

Now that is a great way to cut some stickers for your own needs or as a side business. Some so many people love and use stickers every day.

False Cowhide Home Keychain

Materials

- Cricut Creator
- Faux Calfskin
- Suede
- White Press On Vinyl
- Leather Paste
- Keychain Ring
- Standard Grip Tangle (green)
- Iron or Simple Press

Directions

You'll need to utilize the false cowhide for the house, the calfskin for the heart and the iron-on for "home"

Use cowhide paste to join heart to the fluffy side of the calfskin house that doesn't show some kindness cut out.

Put calfskin stick on the house around the heart and connect the other house, fluffy side down.

Let sit for 30 minutes.

Preheat the false calfskin for 35 seconds before squeezing the home on with the iron or Simple Press.

Put they keychain ring through the entire at the highest point of the house.

Also, much the same as that you have the ideal housewarming present for pretty much anybody!

Calfskin Hair Bow

Materials

- Cricut Investigate

- Faux Calfskin or Cowhide

- Transfer Tape

- Strong Grasp Cricut Tangle

- Bow Cricut Configuration Space Document

- E6000 Paste

- French Barrette Clasps

- Binding Clasps

Instructions

Line your artificial softened cowhide or calfskin with your exchange tape. This will give something for the texture to clutch as opposed to leaving fluff everywhere on your tangle and essentially demolishing it. This was an immense help and I'll never return to staying the texture ideal on the solid hold tangle again.

When you pick the artificial cowhide setting on your Keen Dial, it'll slice through the item twice. At the point when your pictures are excessively near one another, occasionally it will catch and draw the item. To stay away from this, move your pictures promote separated when you're seeing your tangle. This will spare items over the long haul and spare many cerebral pains. Try not to be hesitant to utilize some scissors if you have one knick in the calfskin.

Begin with every one of your pieces laid out. You'll need to overlay the longest piece with the goal that the finishes compromise. Secure that with the E6000 stick and a coupling cut. On the off chance that you've made in excess of one bow, right now is an ideal opportunity to gather all the more drawn out pieces.

Next, you'll assume the back and position some E6000 stick in the center and take your bow piece and hold fast it to that, safe with a coupling cut. Enable it to dry only a couple of minutes in the middle of each progression.

Next, put some E6000 on the barrette and lay the back piece to it. Take your little center piece and apply the paste to that. Overlay it over the bow in the center and around the back of the barrette. Secure that with a coupling cut. I'd permit these to dry for a couple of hours before you stick them in their hair to make sure they don't get any paste on them.

Shamrock Earrings

Materials

- Cricut Maker Earring (from a Cricut Project)

- Rotary Wheel Knife Blade FabricGrip

- Mat StrongGrip Mat Weeder Tool Cricut

- Leather Scraper Tool Adhesive PebbledFaux

- Leather Earring Hooks

Directions

First, open the Cricut Project (Earring). You can now either click on "Make It" or "Customize" to edit it.

Once you've selected one, click on "Continue."

Immediately the Cut page pops up, select your material and wait for the "Load" tools and Mat to appear.

Make your Knife blade your cutting tool in clamp B. This will be used on the Leather.

On the StrongGrip Mat, place the Leather and make sure it's facing down. Then load the Mat into the machine and tap the "Cut" flashing button. When the scoring has been done, go back to the cutting tool and change it to Rotary Wheel so that you can use it on the Faux Leather.

Similarly, place your Faux leather on your FabricGrip Mat, facing down. Then load the Mat into the machine and tap the "Cut" flashing button.

Take away all the items on the Mat with your Scraper tool. Be careful with the small fringes though.

Make a hole on the top circle by making use of the Weeder tool. Make sure the hole is large enough to make the Earring hooks fit in.

If necessary, you may have to twist the hook's end with the pliers to fit them in.

Close them up after you have looped it inside the hole that was made inside the Earring.

Finally, you should glue the Shamrock to the surface of the Earring with adhesive. Wait for it to dry before using it.

Fun Foam Stamps

Want to work on a fun project that any kid would enjoy and that can be completed in no time? This is the perfect project for you then as fun foam stamps are both fun to make and fun to use. You will also get a chance to make something out of craft foam sheets in combination with only a few materials and the inevitable use of your Cricut machine. Let's see how you can make your own fun foam stamps today.

Materials

- Craft Foam Sheets
- Wooden blocks - small blocks, not larger than 4 inches
- Glue
- Cricut machine

Directions

Open your Design Space and go to Images. You can search for the images through the library by using specific words, or browse through the library to find the images you like. You can choose letters as well if you would like to make letter stamps. Numbers can be used as well. You can use fun images of unicorns, hearts, stars, or whichever shape or image you find interesting. Use the top editing panel to size the images for your stamps. Images shouldn't be larger than 2 inches, but you can also make them larger or smaller if you prefer. Make sure to size the images to fit the wooden blocks.

Once you click on "Make it", make sure to set the material to cutting foam as you will be using foam sheets for your designs. You can cut several images at once, while it is handy not to have more than 6 x 2-inch images prepared for cutting. Set your cutting mat and arrange your foam material – you can use different colors for different stamp images. Once you have set up everything, you can start cutting.

Once the images are cut out, you can start gluing them to the wooden blocks. It is best to let the glue dry overnight before you start using stamps. You are all done and good to go!

Personalized Doormat

If personalized crafts with fun designs and witty statements sound tempting, you will love the personalized doormat. Luckily enough, we have the "recipe" for this fine piece of DIY ready for you. Aside from a doormat and your cutting mat, you will need to gather some more supplies, so let's see what you need to start making a personalized doormat to show people your welcome.

Materials

- Heavy cardstock
- Doormat – plain
- Stencil brush
- Tape
- Fabric paint
- Cricut machine
- Gloves are recommended since you will be using fabric paint

Directions

What is important for you to make for this project is the pattern for your doormat - you can use a cute design or go for a witty statement written in a bold and interesting font. You can also download the

SVG file with an already ready design. In case you are uploading the SVG file, you will have fewer steps to complete as you will be able to proceed to cut in only a couple of steps.

In case you are starting from scratch, make sure to create a base element for your design - this would be a layer on which you will place your statement or another cool design. You can choose any font you like, and in case you are searching for an interesting image, you can always browse through the image library. Once you have the design ready, you need to select the layers and click on "Weed". You want to cut and weed the image then remove the negative part - the negative part would be the letters inside your design. You will need the letters to be cut out, so you could make a paint pattern for the doormat.

Once your design is ready and you are happy with the outcome, you can click on the "Make it" button to send your design to cut. Make sure to prepare the material and your mat and set the cutting preferences to heavy cardstock. You will use the heavy cardstock as your stencil. When the cutting is done, take the tape, the paint and the brush alongside your pattern and let's move onto the finishing step.

For the final step, you will carefully glue the edges of the pattern with tape so you can fixate it to the doormat. Take the stencil brush and use it to apply paint over the pattern. Careful not to paint outside the edges of the pattern. Paint over the letters. Let the doormat dry then remove the pattern and wish your visitors a warm welcome with a personalized doormat.

Cricut Bookmarker

Reading books can be even more tempting and interesting with an attractive bookmark to keep you company and help you mark your pages when you want to make a pause. You can easily make a lovely bookmarker and make it personalized with your Cricut machine and this simple project. let's see what you need to start making your first bookmark with the Cricut machine.

Materials

- Scrapbook
- Scrapbook adhesive
- 6-inch twine
- 12-inch ribbon
- Cricut machine

Directions

For the first step, you will find an SVG file you can use for making a bookmark, download it online then upload it to Design Space, or search for different designs in the library of images, paid and free. Another option is to create your own design on Canvas and personalize your bookmark. Whatever option you decide to go for, you need to have your scrapbook paper cut in 6" x 2 1/4" and 5 3/4" x 2". That means that you need to make a layer for your design according to these measures. You can always cut extra length if you would like the bookmarker to be smaller. You want to have two pieces of scrapbook so you can attach them together once the parts are cut. That is how you will make one piece to be 6" x 2 1/4" and the other 5 3/4" x 2" on Design Space as well. You can have different designs for each of the pieces and make sure that colors and designs are a perfect match when combined. You will also create a ¼-inch hole on the top part of the bookmark pieces. You can choose "Shapes" and select the circle. A circle will appear on the canvas. Select the shape and click "Duplicate". Place each circle on the top of the bookmark pieces and adjust the size of the circles. Select the circles and click on "Weld" to cut out the holes. Alternatively, you can use a hole puncher as a tool instead, however, you can do all parts of the project with your Cricut machine.

Once you have the design ready, you can proceed to cut by clicking the "Make it" button. Make sure to select scrapbook paper as your material choice before cutting. Prepare the cutting mat and the material. Cut.

Once you are done with cutting you will need to prepare your paper adhesive, twine, and the ribbon.

First, attach the two pieces of scrapbook paper with paper adhesive. Once the pieces are fixated into one – make sure that the holes you've made on each piece are aligned – you can pull the ribbon through and even it by ends.

Use the twine to tie the ribbon by the edge of the bookmark. There you have it! Your own personalized bookmark! You can use any design you want and try making different bookmarks with or without the ribbons and with different details.

Personalized Phone Case

Using a protective case for your fun can also be a lot of fun – especially with the Cricut machine – you can change designs and refresh the style of your phone with each new phone case project you decide to make. And, you only need a few more things to start aside from your Cricut machine.

Materials

- Foil Adhesive Vinyl
- Transfer tape
- Clear phone case – more room for fun!
- Weeding tool
- Scissors or scalpel
- Cricut machine – Cricut Maker or Cricut Explore Air

Directions

As always when starting out fresh, click on "New Project" to open a blank canvas. You can make this project a breeze by clicking on "Templates". Here you can find templates for numerous different projects, which includes phone cases as well. Choose the phone case template. Make sure to size the template layer to fit the size of the clear phone case you have prepared for the project. From there, you can start working on your design. You can add images of your choice and resize them as needed to make a phone case design. Once your design is ready to go, you will click "Select All" then choose "Attach" option. This will prepare the design for cutting as you need both the phone case rectangle layer cut out and the designs used for the phone case.

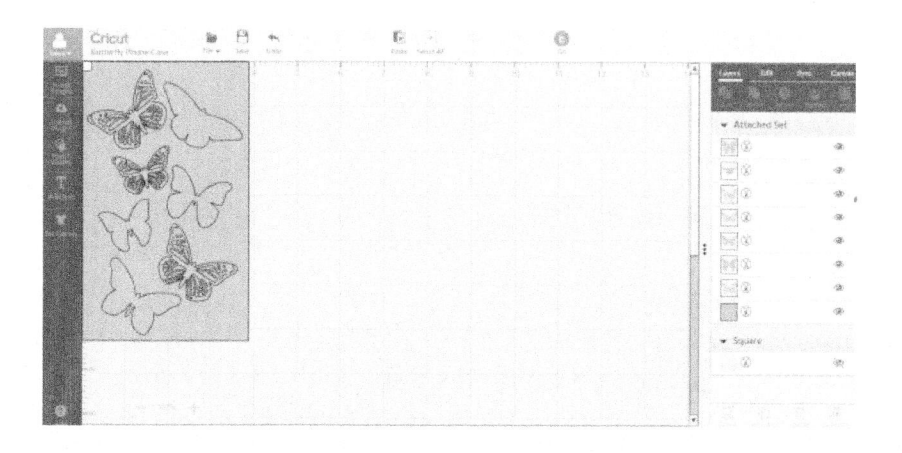

If you are happy with your design you can click on "Make it". Before proceeding with cutting, choose Foil Adhesive Vinyl as your material. Set up the cutting mat and prepare the material to start cutting.

Now that your design is cut out, it's time to use the weeding tool. Remove all excess vinyl from the design - in this case, excess material would be the background while your designs (butterflies for example) should remain intact. Next, attach the transfer tape to the vinyl and remove the backing paper. Attach the vinyl to the phone case with the transfer tape. You will use your scissors or a scalpel to remove the excess part of the vinyl once it is attached to the phone case – remove those parts that don't fit the phone case design. For instance, you will need to remove the part of the vinyl piece covering the camera slot on the phone case. Remove the tape, and voila! You have your own personalized phone case. You can make as many designs as you like using these guidelines.

CHAPTER 5:

Special Occasion Projects

Chipboard Tree Ornaments

Personalized Christmas ornaments are filled with history and memories for a family. With the Cricut, you can make all sorts of Christmas tree ornaments. Once you have mastered the art of making them, get the family involved in decorating them.

Materials

- Cricut glitter adhesive vinyl — red or a selection of colors
- Cricut chipboard
- Green Standard Grip mat
- Purple Strong Grip map
- Cricut Fine-Point Blade
- Cricut Knife Blade
- Weeding tool
- Spatula
- Pair of scissors for cutting the material to size
- Ribbon — red or white
- White matte finish paint
- Builder's tape

Directions

1. Open a new project in Design Space.
2. Select 'Diamond' from the 'Shapes' menu on the left-hand side.

3. Leave the color as the default color.

4. Unlock the shape and change it to 1.969" wide and 3.416" long.

5. Select 'Octagon' from the 'Shapes' menu on the left-hand side.

6. Leave the color as the default color.

7. Leave the shape as the default 3.111" wide and 3.111" long.

8. Select 'Star' from the 'Shapes' menu on the left-hand side.

9. Leave the color as the default color.

10. Leave the shape as the default 3.271" wide and 3.111" long.

11. Select 'Heart' from the 'Shapes' menu on the left-hand side.

12. Leave the color as the default color.

13. Leave the shape as the default 3.282" wide and 3.106" long.

14. Select 'Text' from the menu on the left-hand side.

15. Leave the color as the default color.

16. Choose a nice Christmas font. Balega Std Regular is used as an example for this project. The font size is set to 44.2.

17. Type "Peace" and move the text to the middle of the octagon. Leave some space on either side of the text box.

18. Duplicate the text and move the duplicate text to one side out of the way.

19. Highlight the text and octagon, right-click, and select 'Slice.'

20. Remove the top 2 slices and delete them.

21. Repeat steps 17 to 20 for each shape.

    a. Type "Love" for the heart shape

    b. Type "Joy" for the star shape

    c. Type "Hope" for the diamond shape

22. Select 'Circle' from the 'Shapes' menu on the left-hand side.

23. Leave the color as the default color.

24. Leave the shape as the default 0.306" wide and 0.306" long.

25. Make four duplicates of the small circle.

26. Position one circle on the left round part of the heart shape.

27. Select the circle and the heart, right-click, and select 'Slice.'

28. Remove and delete the top 2 slices.

29. Repeat steps 26 to 28 for the right round part of the heart shape.

30. Position one circle on the top point of the star shape.

31. Select the circle and the star, right-click, and select 'Slice.'

32. Remove and delete the top 2 slices.

33. Repeat steps 30 to 32 for the rest of the shapes, positioning the circle at the top in the middle of each.

34. Click 'Make it.'

35. You can fit at least 2 of each shape onto one board.

36. Set 'Project copies' to 2 and click 'Apply.'

37. Position the objects on the page so they are not touching.

38. Set the Cricut blade to the fine-point blade and print out the glitter vinyl copies first.

39. Each ornament will need two vinyl overlays, one for each side. It is suggested to have one side in red glitter vinyl and the other side in green glitter vinyl.

40. Once the glitter vinyl copies have finished cutting, set the Cricut blade to the knife blade and use the purple mat.

41. Remember to stick the chipboard down with builder's tape to keep it steady.

42. While the chipboard is being cut, weed the vinyl overlays and get them ready.

43. When the chipboard has finished being cut, remove the ornaments from the mat.

44. Clean the shapes and text.

45. Paint them on both sides and the edges with the white matte or chalk finish paint.

46. Leave the ornaments to completely dry.

47. When the ornaments are dry, carefully transfer the glitter vinyl onto them.

48. Cut pieces of ribbon and tie it through the little holes on the top of the ornaments.

49. They are ready to hang on the tree.

Easter Basket Fun

Christmas is not the only time for decorations! Here's a great suggestion for how to liven up the Easter holidays.

Materials

- Pink Cricut cardstock
- Blue Cricut cardstock
- Pink Cricut glitter tape
- Clear Cricut sticker paper
- Green Standard Grip mat
- Cricut Fine-Point Blade
- Stylus scoring pen or wheel

- Weeding tool

- Scraping tool or brayer tool

- Pair of scissors for cutting the material to size

- Inkjet printer

- Glue dots or hot glue gun

Directions

1. Open a new project in Design Space.

2. Select 'Pentagon' from the 'Shapes' menu on the left-hand side.

3. Change the background color to blue.

4. Leave the shape as the default size.

5. Select 'Square' from the 'Shapes' menu on the left-hand side.

6. Leave the background color as the default color.

7. Unlock the shape and change it to 3.375" wide and 3.139" long.

8. Move the pentagon to the following position on the screen: x = 1.986 and y = 1.833

9. Move the square over the top point of the pentagon in the following position on the screen: x = 1.972 and y = 0

10. Select the square and the pentagon. To not disturb the slice, select the objects from the 'Layers' panel on the right-hand side of the screen.

11. Select the 2 objects by first selecting the square, holding down the <Ctrl> key on the keyboard, then selecting the pentagon.

12. Right-click and select 'Slice.'

13. Remove all the slices and delete them.

14. Remove the 2 triangle objects but do not delete them; instead, move them out of the way.

15. Change the sliced pentagon to the following size: width = 5.75" and height = 2.724".

16. Select 'Square' from the 'Shapes' menu on the left-hand side.

17. Change the background color to blue.

18. Unlock the shape and change it to 3.111" wide and 2.724" long.

19. Create a duplicate of the square.

20. Unlock the duplicate square and change it to 4.724" wide and 4.724" long.

21. Move the larger square to the following position on the screen: x = 4.306 and y = 3.361

22. Move the pentagon to the following position on the screen: x = 2.955 and y = 0.611

23. Move the smaller square to the following position on the screen: x = 5.917 and y = 0.611

24. Select the pentagon shape and the smaller square shape, right-click, and select 'Weld.' This is the box's side.

25. Select 'Score Line' from the 'Shapes' menu on the left-hand side.

26. Unlock the shape and change the height to 2.724".

27. Move the score line to the following position on the screen: x = 4.333 and y = 0.847

28. Create a duplicate of the score line and move over to the side.

29. Swivel the score line so it runs horizontally.

30. Unlock the shape and change it to 3.111" width.

31. Move the score line to the following position on the screen: x = 4.306 and y = 3.361.

32. Select the box side and the 2 score lines, right-click, and select 'Attach.'

33. Create 3 duplicates of the box side with score lines.

34. Rotate each of the box sides and fit them together around the square.

35. When all the sides are attached to the square, it will resemble a flattened box.

36. Select 'Square' from the 'Shapes' menu on the left-hand side.

37. Change the background color to pink.

38. Unlock the shape and change it to 3.111" width and 2.724" length.

39. Select 'Images' from the menu on the left-hand side.

40. Change the background color to pink.

41. Find an image of bunny ears. This project uses #M8620AE4 as an example.

42. Unlock the shape and change it to 1.276" wide and 1.168" long.

43. Create a duplicate of the bunny ears.

44. Move the one bunny ears over the top of the pink square.

45. Flip the duplicate of the bunny ears vertically and attach the image to the bottom of the pink rectangle.

46. Select the pink square and both bunny ear images, right-click, and select 'Attach.'

47. Select 'Score Line' from the 'Shapes' menu on the left-hand side.

48. Unlock the shape and change the height to 0.847".

49. Swivel the score line so it runs horizontally.

50. Create a duplicate of the score line and move it over to the side.

51. Move the one score line to just below the bunny ears on the top of the pink rectangle. It must fit perfectly into the pink square.

52. Do the same for the second score line at the bottom of the pink rectangle.

53. Select the pink rectangle and the score lines, right-click, and select 'Attach.'

54. **Save the project.**

55. Make sure the scoring stylus is loaded into the Cricut.

56. Set the Cricut dial to cardstock.

57. In Design Space, click 'Make it.'

58. Position the box on the mat so it fits with enough bleed around the edges of the cutting board.

59. Make sure the bunny handle is not flush against the side of the pink cutting board.

60. Load the appropriate color material, which is going to be blue cardstock for the basket and pink cardstock for the bunny handle.

61. When the basket and handle have printed, use the glue dots to glue the basket sides together.

62. Where each side of the box folds into the other, you will need to make a small snip at the bottom to free the fold.

63. When the basket is assembled, stick the pink Cricut glitter ribbon around it.

64. Fold the bunny ears on the bottom of the handle up against the rectangle and glue them into position.

65. Where the bunny ears fold up onto the handle will be where you will stick the hand onto the basket.

66. Fill with Easter goodies.

Valentine's Gift Tags

In a few steps, you can create this easy I Love You Gift with Cricut. Make a donation tag or stack.

I have a canvas of Design Space, click and create.

You can customize the look of the Valentine Cricut project by replacing your cutting materials, selecting your favorite colors to go with a fun fabric.

You can also flatten the entire design piece into a multitude of Cricut Projects print-then-cut.

Materials

- Cricut Machine Design Space
- Account Variety of card inventory
- Gold pen
- Cut designs you need to create this I Love You gift tag with your Cricut

Directions

1. Follow on-screen instructions to draw and cut each layer as required.

2. Glue the two layers of paper together, aligning the heart-shaped hole atop the tag.

3. Add the vinyl and burn to guarantee it adheres carefully. I can't apply vinyl, particularly glitter vinyl. You can attempt using the transfer tape, but the glitter tends not to stick to the transfer tape.

4. Add twine or ribbon to the tag and attach the tag as you like. You can use the tag back to write a unique signal to someone.

5. Alternatively, instead of using glue, you can bind the two cutouts together. Add these Valentine tags in your charms, embellishments, and fun accents.

6. Draw a beautiful accent design with your gold glitter pen. Add glitter vinyl word art to your Valentine tag

7. You can use this pleasant Valentine's Day Cricut project to produce all kinds of custom tags or use parts to make other types of projects. Change colors, materials, and wording.

Halloween T-Shirt

Materials

1. T-shirt Blanks

2. Glam Halloween SVG Files

3. Cardstock

4. Transfer Sheets (Black and Pink)

5. Butcher Paper (comes with Infusible Ink rolls)

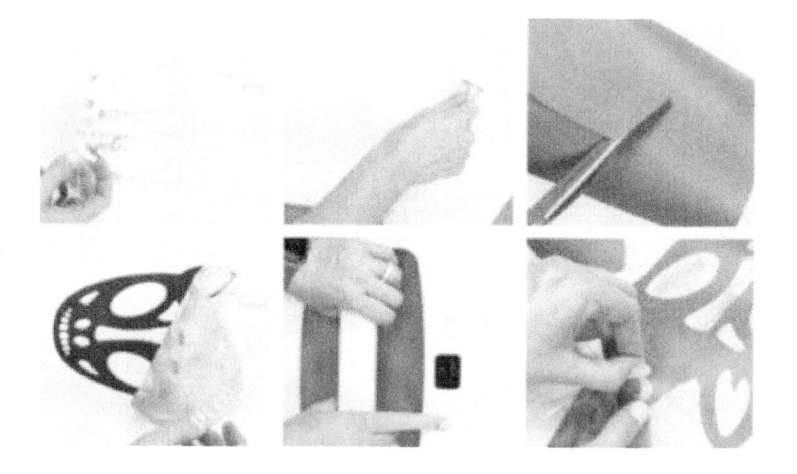

Directions

1. Import the SVG files into Cricut Design Space and arrange them as you want them on the T-shirt.

2. Change the sizes of the designs so as to get them to fit on the T-shirt.

3. Using the slice tool, slice the pink band away from the hat's bowler part (the largest piece). Make a copy of this band, and then slice it from the lower part of the hat. With these done, you will have three pieces that fit together.

4. You can change the designs' colors as you would like them. When you are done with the preparation, click "Make It."

5. Ensure that you invert your image using the "Mirror" toggle. This is even more important if there is text on your design, as infusible ink designs should be done in inverse. This is because the part with the ink is to go right on the destination material.

6. For the material, select Infusible ink. After this, cut the design out using your Cricut Machine.

7. With the designs cut out, weed the transfer sheet.

8. Cut around the designs such that the transfer tape does not cover any part of the infusible ink sheet. Make sure that this is done well as any part of the infusible ink that is not in contact with the fabric will not be transferred.

9. Preheat your EasyPress to 385°, and set your EasyPress mat.

10. Prepare your T-shirt by placing it on the EasyPress mat, then using a lint roller to remove any lint from the front.

11. Insert the Cardstock in the t-shirt, between the front and back, just where the design will be. This will protect the other side of the T-shirt from having the Infusible Ink on it.

12. To layer colors, ensure that your cutting around the transfer sheet is done as close as possible, then repeat the previous three steps for each color. This will prevent the transfer sheet from removing part of the color on the previously transferred design.

No-Sew Felt Nativity Finger Puppets

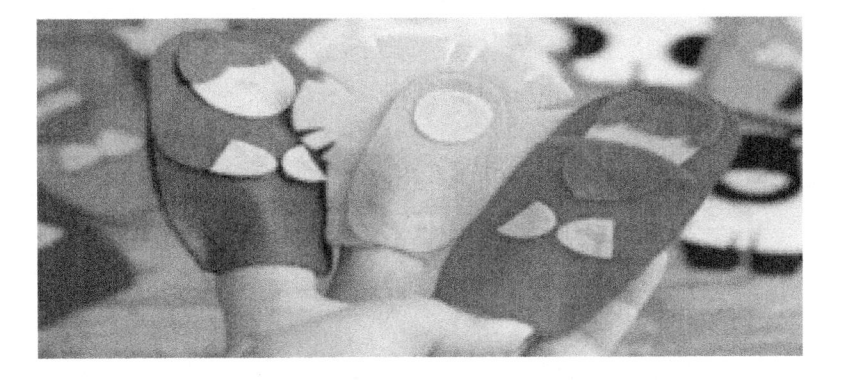

Utilize your Cricut Creator to make this charming no-sew felt Nativity finger manikins.

On the off chance that you don't have kids of your own, I think these would influence an awesome Christmas to present for neighbors with kids or grandchildren.

Materials

- Cricut Producer
- Rotary Edge (accompanies Cricut Producer)
- Cricut Felt Sky Sampler
- Cricut Felt Merry go round Sampler
- Cricut Fabric Grip Tangle
- Hot stick weapon and paste sticks

Directions

1. Open Cricut Configuration Space and open this record —> Nativity Finger Manikins

2. Click on "Make" It and Select "Felt" as the Material to cut. Load your rotational edge into your machine and load the relating shade of felt appeared on the Outline Screen on to your Cricut Fabric Grip Tangle.

3. Once you have removed the majority of your mats, precisely amass every one of the manikins together to get together.

4. Using your heated glue weapon, make a line of paste around the back of the finger manikin. Lay the front piece to finish everything and press to anchor. At that point stick the other manikin pieces, for example, hair, face and arms on. Rehash with every manikin. You will dependably complete a finger molded line of paste on the back bit of the manikin.

5. Presently your manikins are finished! Give those little fingers a chance to play away with their own Nativity.

CHAPTER 6:

How To Start Selling Your Project

It is a well-known fact in the world of business that to make money, you first need to invest money. With that being said, if you already own a Cricut cutting machine, then you can jump to the next paragraph, but if you are debating if it's worth the investment, then read on. As mentioned earlier, Cricut has a range of cutting machines with distinctive capabilities offered at a varying price range. The Cricut Explore Air 2 is priced at $249.99, and the Cricut Maker is priced at $399.99 (the older Cricut Explore Air model may be available for sale on Amazon at a lower price). Now, if you were to buy any of these machines during a holiday sale with a bundle deal that comes with a variety of tools, accessories, and materials for a practice project as well as free trial membership to Cricut Access, you would already be saving enough to justify the purchase for your personal usage. The cherry on top would be if you can use this investment to make more money. You can always get additional supplies in a bundle deal or from your local stores at a much lower price. All in all, those upfront costs can easily be justified with the expenses you budget for school projects that require you to cut letters and shapes, create personalized gifts for your loved ones, decorate your home with customized decals, and of course, your own jewelry creations. These are only a handful of the reasons to buy a Cricut machine for your personal use. Let's start scraping the mountain of Cricut created wealth to help you get rich while enjoying your work!

At this stage, let's assume that you have bought a Cricut cutting machine and have enough practice with the beginner-friendly projects. You now have the skillset and the tools to start making money with your Cricut machine, so let's jump into how you can make it happen. The ways listed below have been tried and tested as successful money-making strategies that you can implement with no hesitations.

Selling Pre-Cut Customized Vinyl

Vinyl is super beginner friendly material to work with and comes in a variety of colors and patterns to add to its great reputation. You can create customized labels for glass containers and canisters to help anyone looking to organize their pantry. Explore the online trends and adjust the labels. Once you have your labels designed, the easiest approach is to set up an "Etsy" shop, which is free and very easy to use. It's almost like opening an Amazon prime membership account. If your design is in demand, you will have people ordering even with no advertising. But if you would like to keep the tempo high, then advertise your Etsy listing on Pinterest and other social media platforms. This is a sure-shot way to generate more traffic to your Etsy shop and to turn potential customers into paying customers. An important note here is the pictures being used on your listing. You cannot use any of the stock images from the Design Space application and must use your own pictures that match the product you are selling.

Create a package of 5 or 6 different labels like sugar, salt, rice, oats, beans, etc. that can be sold as a standard packager and offer a customized package that will allow the customer to request any word that they need to be included in their set. Since these labels weigh next to nothing, shipping can easily be managed with standard mail with usually only a single postage stamp, depending on the delivery address. Make sure you do not claim the next day or two-day delivery for these. Build enough delivery time so you can create and ship the labels without any stress. Once you have an established business model, you can adjust the price and shipping of your product, but more on that later. Check out other Etsy listings to make sure your product pricing is competitive enough, and you are attracting enough potential buyers.

Now, once you have traction in the market, you can offer additional vinyl-based projects like bumper stickers, iron-on, or heat transfer vinyl designs that people can transfer on their clothing using a standard heating iron. Really, once you have gained some clientele, you can modify and customize all your listings to develop into a one-stop-shop for all things vinyl (great name for your future Etsy shop, right!).

Selling Finished Pieces

You would be using your Cricut machines for a variety of personal projects like home décor, holiday décor, personalized clothing, and more. Next time you embark on another one of your creative journeys leading to unique creations, just make two of everything, and you can easily put the other product to sell on your Etsy shop. Another great advantage is that you will be able to save all your projects on the Design Space application for future use, so if one of your projects goes viral, you can easily buy the supplies and turn them into money-making offerings. This way, not only your original idea for personal usage will be paid off, but you can make much more money than you invested in it, to begin with.

Again, spend some time researching what kind of designs and decorations are trending in the market and use them to spark up inspiration for your next project. Some of the current market trends include customized cake and cupcake toppers and watercolor designs that can be framed as fancy wall decorations. The cake toppers can be made with cardstock, which is another beginner-friendly material, light in weight, and can be economically shipped tucked inside an envelope.

Personalized Clothing and Accessories

T-shirts with cool designs and phrases are all the rage right now. Just follow a similar approach to the selling vinyl section and take it up a notch. You can create sample clothing with iron-on design and market it with "can be customized further at no extra charge" or "transfer the design on your own clothing" to get traction in the market. You can buy sling bags and customize them with unique designs to be sold as finished products at a higher price than a plain boring sling bag. Consider creating a line of products with a centralized theme like the DC Marvel characters or the Harry Potter movies and design custom t-shirts, hats, and even bodysuits for babies. You can create customized party favor boxes and gift bags at the request of the customer. Once your product has a dedicated customer base, you can get project ideas from them directly and quote them a price for your work. Isn't that great?!?!

Another big advantage of the heat transfer vinyl, as mentioned earlier, is that anyone can transfer the design on their desired item of clothing using a standard household iron. But you would need to include the transfer instructions with the order letting them know exactly how to prep for the heat transfer without damaging their chosen clothing item. And again, heat transfer vinyl can be easily shipped using a standard mailing envelope. We have added a dedicated section on tips for using everyday iron-on with a household iron.

Marketing on Social Media

We are all aware of how social media has become a marketing platform for not only established corporations, but also small businesses and budding entrepreneurs. Simply add hashtags like for sale, product, selling, free shipping, sample included, and more to entice potential buyers. Join Facebook community pages and groups for handcraft sellers and buyers to market your products. Use catchy phrases like customization available at no extra cost or free returns if not satisfied when posting the products on these pages as well as your personal Facebook page. Use Twitter to share feedback from your satisfied customers to widen your customer base. You can do this by creating a satisfaction survey that you can email to your buyers or include a link to your Etsy listing asking for online reviews and ratings from your customers.

Another tip here is to post pictures of anything and everything you have created using Cricut machines, even those that you did not plan to sell. You never know who else might need something that you deemed unsellable. Since you will be creating these only after the order has been placed, you can easily gather the required supplies after the fact and get crafting.

Target Local Farmer's Market And Boutiques

If you like the thrill of a show-and-tell, then reserve a booth at a local farmer's market and show up with some ready to sell crafts. In this case, you are relying on the number of people attending and a subset of those who might be interested in making a purchase from you. If you are in an urban neighborhood where people are keenly interested in unique art designs but do not have the time to create them on their own, you can easily make big bucks by setting a decent price point for your products.

Bring flyers to hand out people so they can reach you through one of your social media accounts or email and check all your existing Etsy listings. Think of these events as a means of marketing for those who are not as active online but can be excited with customized products to meet their next big life event like baby shower, birthday party, or a wedding.

One downside to participating in local events is the generation of mass inventory and booth displays, topped with expenses to load and transport the inventory. You may or may not be able to sell all of the inventory depending on the size of the event, but as I said earlier, you can still make the most of this by marketing your products and building up a local clientele.

CHAPTER 7:

Maintenance Of Your Cricut Machine

The Cricut Cutter machine needs to be kept intact in a variety of ways: the blade must be replaced, the cutting mats must be taken care of, and the machine, in general, must be kept clean.

Cutting Blade

Every single blade you use might get up to fifteen thousand individual cuts before it needs to be replaced. To prolong this number of individual cuts, place the aluminum foil onto the cutting mat and cut out a few designs. This process keeps the blade extra sharp and lengthens the life of the blade. This number of cuts can be greatly based on what types of materials that have been cut by the blade. If you are doing many projects in which thick materials need to be cut the blade will deteriorate quickly; the blade can also deteriorate quickly if you are cutting many materials on high pressure. A good way to know if your blade needs to be replaced is if the quality of your cuts starts to greatly decrease. If this happens it's best to replace the cutting blade. When replacing the blade, it is always best to get blades that are Cricut brand. Generic blades are often not the best quality and will cause you to constantly replace your cutting blade. To install the new blade once you've ordered the correct one, you need to first unplug your Cricut Cutter machine. Always unplug the machine before installing anything in your Cricut cutter. Next, you must remove the old, dull cutting blade from your Cricut Cutter machine. Once the cutting blade assembly has been separated it is now time to eject the blade. Find the small silver button above the adjustment knob and press the button down; this will eject the cutting blade. Be very, very careful when doing this as the blade is extremely sharp and can easily cut through the skin. Keep all blades away from children and pets. To put in the new blade, insert the blade on the end of the blade assembly opposite of the blade release button. The blade will then be pulled up into the assembly. Place the assembly back into the machine by reversing the process.

Subscribe to Cricut Access

If you really want to get a full range of use out of both your Cricut Explore machine as well as the Cricut Maker machine, we would recommend you subscribe to Cricut Access right away. There are two options for payment. You can either pay a monthly fee of $10, or you can pay one time for the entire year. This works out to be slightly cheaper on a month to month basis. This will give you access to thousands of different predesigned projects as well as Cricut Access exclusive fonts, that you would otherwise have to pay to use. If you are planning to use your Cricut a lot, this will save you a lot of money as opposed to buying every project an image individually. We can all agree it is a lot easier to pay one flat rate instead of having to figure out how much you are actually spending on projects. Get your money's worth out of your Cricut and subscribe to Cricut Access.

De-tack Your Cutting Mat

The Circuit Explore machine will come with a green 12"x12" Standard grip cutting mat. The Cricut Maker machine will come with a blue light grip mat. As you already know, you will place your cutting material onto this mat before inserting it into the machine to cut. As you will come to find out, the green cutting mat is extremely sticky when it is brand new.

Keep Your Cutting Mat Covers

The cutting mats that you purchase for your projects will always come brand new with a plastic protecting sheet over it. This can be pulled off and put back on for the entire life of the mat. You will want to keep this plastic cover as long as you have the mat. It will keep the stickiness level up on your mat, and it will make the mat easier to store away when not in use.

Cutting Mat

The Cutting mat in addition to the cutting blade needs to be taken care of. One cutting mat can have a life of anywhere from twenty-five to forty cuts. The life of the cutting mat can vary from this amount depending on the pressure and speed at which the cuts have been made and it the type of materials that have been cut on the mat. To prolong the life of your cutting mat, remove any debris from the mat after a cut and always avoid scraping the mat. If you scrape the mat, it can push any debris further into the mat. After each craft, it is best to run lukewarm water over the mat and dab it dry with a towel afterward. When a material can do not adhere to the cutting mat any longer then it is time to finally replace the mat. It is recommended to get many cutting mats and rotate between them to prolong the life of all the cutting mats. This extends the life of the mats because one cutting mat will not be cut on for many, many projects in a small amount of time. It is also recommended that you keep all of your cutting mats and all of your cartridges and blades in a very organized manner. Throwing the components of haphazardly can destroy and deteriorate them so it is best to keep them in a very organized fashion. A benefit of keeping your Cricut Cutter components organized is you won't lose or damage the very expensive items that are necessary for several projects.

How to Clean a Cricut Mat

Sometimes it also depends on the materials you use that make your machine dirty. For example, using felt means you'd need to grab stray pieces using tweezers. Another great way to clean your Cricut machine is to use a lint roller across the entire machine to pick up debris, scrap vinyl, and pieces of felt. You can also use this roller on your mats.

To clean your mats, if there are any leftover residue on your mats, the general rule is to use bleach and alcohol-free baby wipes to gently wipe the mat clean and remove it from grime, glue, and dust. You can also get yourself GOO GONE. Spray this on your mat and let it sit for 15 minutes, then use a scraper tool to remove the adhesive. But do this only if your mat is very dirty. Otherwise, wet wipes will do. Another tip to keep your mats clean is by putting a protective cover back over them when you are not using them.

Cleaning the Cricut Machine

The final thing to keep clean is the actual Cricut Cutter machine. The machine needs to be wiped down with a damp cloth. Only wipe down the external panels of the machine and with the machine unplugged. Always wipe down the machine with a dry cloth after cleaning the outside of the machine. Never clean the Cricut Cutter machine with abrasive cleaners such as acetone, benzene, and all other alcohol-based cleaners. Abrasive cleaning tools should never be used on the Cricut Cutter machine either. In addition, never submerge any component of the machine or the Cricut Cutter machine into the water as it can damage the machine. Always keep the Cricut Cutter machine away from all foods, liquids, pets, and children. Keep the Cricut Cutter machine in a very dry and dust free environment. Finally, do not put the Cricut Cutter machine in excessive heat, excessive cold, sunlight, or any area where the plastic or any other components on the Cricut Cutter machine can melt.

Cleaning and Care

Cleaning your machine is very important, and you should do it regularly to keep everything in tip-top shape.

If you don't take care of your machine, that's just money down the drain.

But what can you do to care for your machine?

Be gentle with your machine. Remember, it is a machine, so you'll want to make sure that you do take some time and try to keep it nice and in order. Don't be rough with it, and when working with the machine parts, don't be too rough with them, either.

Caring for your machine isn't just about making sure that the parts don't get dirty, but you should also make sure that you keep everything in good working order.

Ensure your machine is on stable footing.

This may seem pretty basic, but ensuring that your machine is on a level surface will allow it to make more precise cuts every single time. Rocking of the machine or wobbling could cause unstable results in your projects.

Ensure no debris has gotten stuck under the feet of your machine that could cause instability before proceeding to the next troubleshooting step!

Redo all Cable Connections

So your connections are in the best possible working order, undo all your cable connection, blow into the ports or use canned air, and then securely plug everything back into the right ports. This will help to make sure all the connections are talking to each other where they should be!

Completely Dust and Clean Your Machine

Your little Cricut works hard for you! Return the favor by making sure you're not allowing gunk, dust, grime, or debris to build up in the surfaces and crevices. Adhesive can build up on the machine around the mat input and on the rollers, so be sure to focus on those areas!

Check Your Blade Housing

Sometimes debris and leavings from your materials can build up inside the housings for your blades! Open them up and clear any built-up materials that could be impeding swiveling or motion.

Sharpen Your Blades

A very popular Cricut trick in use is to stick a clean, fresh piece of foil to your Cricut mat, and run it through with the blade you wish to sharpen. Running the blades through the thin metal helps to revitalize their edges and give them a little extra staying power until it's time to buy replacements.

Cleaning the Machine Itself

In general, the exterior is pretty easy to clean – you just need a damp cloth. Make sure that you never put any machine components in water.

Always disconnect the power before cleaning, as you would with any machine.

Sometimes, grease can build up – you may notice this on the cartridge bar if you use cartridges a lot.

Greasing the Machine

If you need to grease your machine, first make sure that it's turned off and the smart carriage is moved to the left. Use a tissue to wipe this down, and then move it to the right, repeating the process again.

From there, move the carriage to the center and open up a lubrication package. Put a small amount onto a Q-tip.

Never use spray cleaner directly on the machine, for obvious reasons. The bar holding the housing shouldn't be wiped down, but if you do notice an excessive grease, please take the time to make sure that it's cleaned up. Remember to never touch the gear chain near the back of this unit, either, and never clean with the machine on, for your own safety.

Cricut machines are great, but you need to take care in making sure that you keep everything in rightful order.

CHAPTER 8:

Complex Operations

Cricut machines are pretty straightforward with what you need to do in order to make simple designs, but you might wonder about some of the more complex operations. Here, we'll tell you how to accomplish these with just a few simple button presses.

Blade Navigation and Calibration

The blades that come with a Cricut machine are important to understand, and you will need to calibrate your blades every single time you use your machine.

Each blade needs this because it will help you figure out which level of depth and pressure your cut needs to be. Typically, each blade needs to be calibrated only once, which is great, because then you don't have to spend time doing this each time. Once you've done it once, it will stay calibrated, but if you decide to change the housings of the blades or if you use them in another machine, you'll need to calibrate it again.

So, if you plan on using a knife blade and then a rotary blade, you'll want to make sure that you do recalibrate – and make sure you do this before you start with your project. It is actually incredibly easy to do this though, which is why it's encouraged.

To calibrate a blade, you just launch the Design Space, and from there, you open the menu and choose calibration. Then, choose the blade that you're going to put in. For the purpose of this explanation, let's say you're using a knife blade.

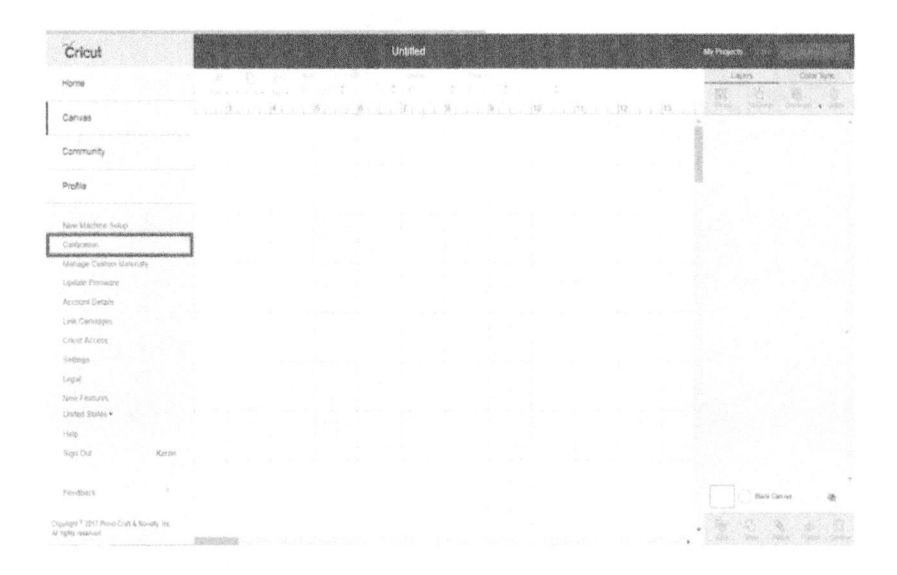

Put that blade in the clamp B area and do a test cut, such as with copy paper into the mat, and then load that into the machine.

Press continue, then press the go button on the machine. It will then do everything that you need for the item itself, and it will start to cut.

You can then choose which calibration is best for your blade, but usually, the first one is good enough.

You can do this with every blade you use, and every time you use a new blade on your machine, I highly recommend you do this – for best results, of course.

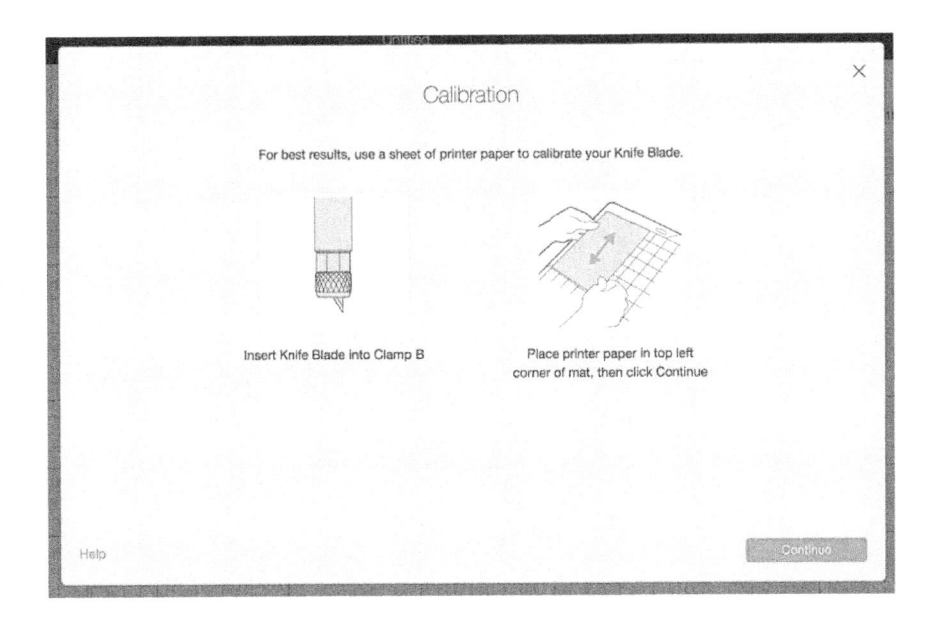

Set Paper Size

Setting paper size in a Cricut machine is actually pretty simple. You will want to use this with either cartridge or with Design Space for what you'd like to make. This also comes with a cutting mat, and you'll want to load this up with paper so that you can use it.

To do this, you'll want to make sure that you have it plugged in, then go to the project preview screen. If you choose a material that's bigger than the mat size, it will automatically be changed, and it'll be adjusted as necessary based on the size of the material that you select.

You can choose the color, the size of the material, whether or not it'll mirror – and you can also choose to fully skip the mat, too, if you don't want that image printed just yet.

Note that the material size menu does offer sizes that are bigger than the largest mat available.

If you're planning on using the print then cut mode, do understand that it's limited to a print area of 8.5x11 inches, but again, you can choose these settings for yourself.

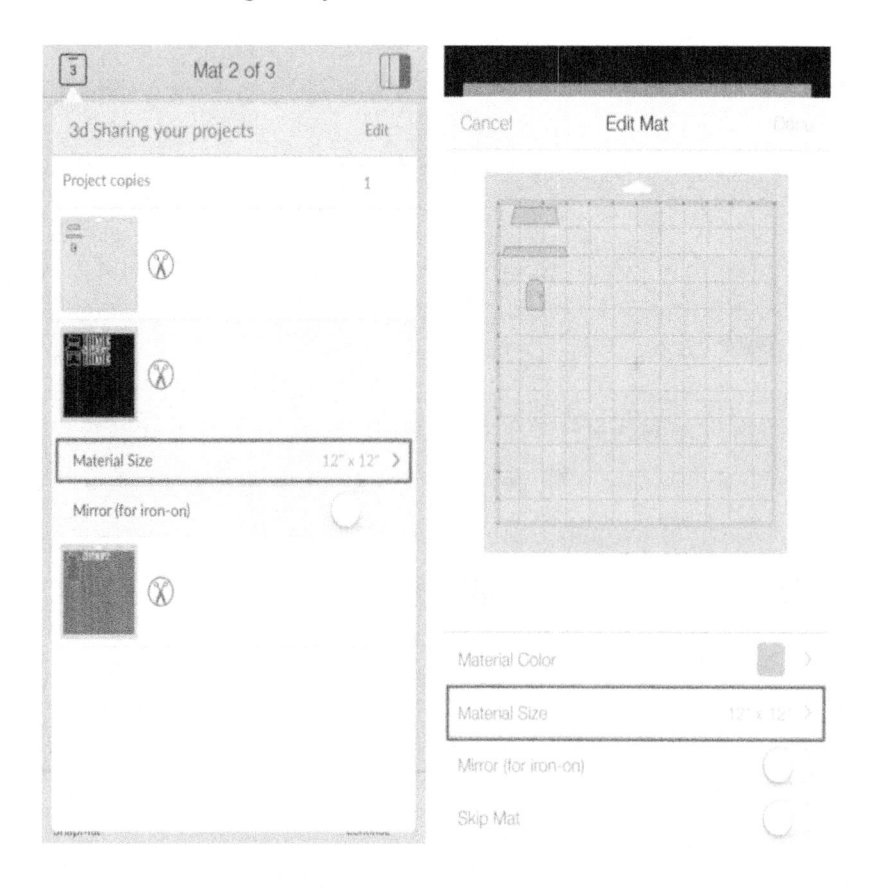

Load Last

To load that paper and image last is pretty simple., press that, and then go. You'll be able to skip this quite easily. It's one of those operations that's definitely a little different from what you may be used to, but if you want to skip design and don't want to work with it just yet, this is probably the best option for you to use. If you're worried about forgetting it, don't worry – Cricut will remind you.

Paper Saver

Saving paper is something you'll want to consider doing with a Cricut machine because it loves to eat up the paper before you even start decorating.

The Explore Air 2 definitely will appreciate it if you save paper, and there are a few ways to do so.

The first one is, of course, to halve your mats. But you don't need to do only that.

You can also go to the material saver option on the machine, which will automatically adjust and align your paper as best it can. Unfortunately, on newer machines, it's actually not directly stated, but there is a way to save paper on these.

You'll want to create tabbed dividers to organize your projects and save them directly there.

The first step is to create a background shape. Make sure that the paper looks like a background. Go to shapes, and then select the square to make the square shape.

Next, once you've created squares to represent the paper, arrange this to move to the back so that the shapes are organized to save the most space on each mat. Then organize the items that are on top of where the background is and arrange them so they all fit on a singular mat.

Rotating is your best friend – you can use this feature whenever you choose objects, so I do suggest getting familiarized with it.

Next, you hide the background at this point, and you do this by choosing the square, and in Design Space, literally hiding this on the right side. Look at the eyeball on the screen, and you'll see a line through the eyeball. That means it's hidden.

Check over everything and fine-tune it at this point. Make sure they're grouped around one object, and make sure everything has measurements. Move these around if they're outside of the measurements required. Once they're confirmed, you then attach these together on the right-hand side of Design Space, which keeps everything neatly together – they're all cut from the same sheet.

From here, repeat this until everything is neatly attached. It will save your paper, but will it save you time? That's debatable, of course.

Speed Dial

So, the speed dial typically comes into play when you're setting the pressure and speed. Fast mode is one of the options available on the Explore Air 2 and the Maker machines, which make the machine run considerably faster than other models. You can use this with vinyl, cardstock, and iron-on materials. To set this, go to the cut screen. You'll have a lot of speed dials here, and various different settings. If you have the right material in place when choosing it, you'll be given the option to do it quickly with fast mode. From there, you simply tap or click on that switch in order to toggle this to the position for on. That will activate fast mode for that item. It will make everything about two times faster, which means that if you're making complex swirl designs, it will take 30 seconds instead of the 73-second average it usually takes. However, one downside to this is that because it's so fast, it will sometimes make the cuts less precise – you'll want to move back to the regular mode for finer work.

This is all usually set with the smart-set dial, which will offer the right settings for you to get the best cuts that you can on any material you're using. Essentially, this dial eliminates you having to manually check the pressure on this. To change the speed and pressure for a particular material that isn't already determined with the preset settings, you will need to select custom mode and choose what you want to create. Of course, the smart-set dial is better for the Cricut products and mats. If you notice that the blade is cutting too deep or not deep enough, there is a half-settings option on each material that you can adjust to achieve the ideal cut. Usually, the way you do this with the pre-set settings is to upload and create a project, press go, and load the mat, then move the smart-set dial on the machine itself to any setting. Let's select custom and choose the speed for this one. In Design Space, you then choose the material, add the custom speed, and you can adjust these settings. You can even adjust the number of times you want the cut to be changed with the smart-set dial, too. Speed is something you can adjust to suit the material, which can be helpful if you're struggling with putting together some good settings for your items.

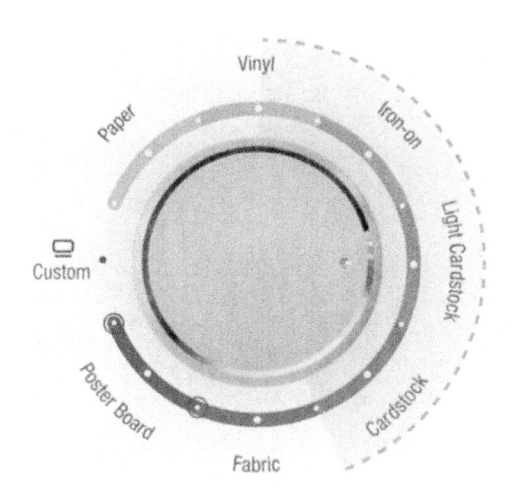

Pressure Dial

Now, let's talk about pressure. Each piece of material will require different pressure settings. If you're not using enough pressure, the blade won't cut into the material, and if you use too much pressure, you'll end up cutting the mat, which isn't what you want to do. The smart-set dial kind of takes the guesswork out of it. You simply choose the setting that best fits your material, and from there, you let it cut. If you notice you're not getting a deep enough cut, then you'll want to adjust it about half a setting to get a better result. From there, adjust as needed. But did you know that you can change the pressure on the smart-set dial for custom materials? Let's say you're cutting something that's very different, such as foil, and you want to set the pressure to be incredibly light so that the foil doesn't get shredded. What you do is you load the material in, and you choose the custom setting. You can then choose the material you plan to cut, such as foil – and if it's not on the list, you can add it.

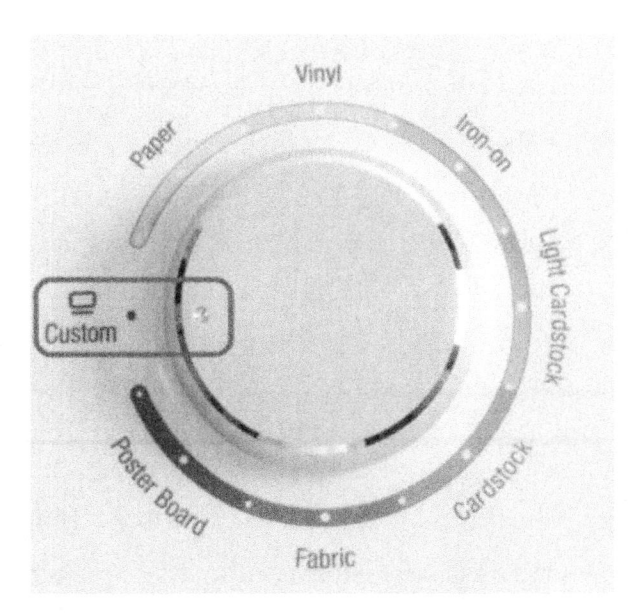

From here, you're given pressure options. Often, people will go too heavy with their custom settings, so I do suggest that you go lighter for the first time and change it as needed. There is a number of draggers that goes from low to high. If you need lots of pressure, obviously let it go higher.

If you don't need much pressure, make sure it's left lower. You will also want to adjust the number of times the cut is done on a multi-cut feature item.

This is a way for you to achieve multiple cuts for the item, which can be incredibly helpful for those who are trying to get the right cut, or if the material is incredibly hard to cut.

I don't suggest using this for very flimsy and thin material, because it'll just waste your blade and the mat itself.

That's all there is to it! This is a great way to improve on your Cricut designs. Personally, I love to work with custom cuts, and you can always delete these if you feel like they don't work. You just press the change settings button to adjust your pressure, speed, or how many cuts you want, and then choose to save when you're done.

What if you don't like a setting, period? You can delete it, of course!

To delete, go to materials settings, and you'll see a little trash can next to it. Press the trash can, and the setting will be removed.

Adjusting the pressure and cuts is part of why people love using Design Space, and it's a great feature to try.

Cricut Design Space

Design Space lets you do many things with your Cricut machine. Here are a few things you can do with this convenient app:

- Aligning various items right next to one another.

- Attaching items to hold images in place, and lets you use score lines.

- Arranging these to make them sit on the canvas in different layers.

- Canvas, a tool that lets you arrange prints and vectors so you can use the various tools with them.

- Contouring, which is a tool that lets you hide image layers quickly, so they're not cut out.

- Color sync, which lets you use multiple colors in one project to reduce the material differences.

- Cut buttons, which will start cuts.

- Make it button: this is the screen that lets you see the designs being cut.

- Draw lines: lets you draw with the pen to write images and such.

- Fill: lets you fill in a pattern or color on an item.

- Flipping items flip it horizontally or vertically by 180 degrees.

- Group: puts different text and images on a singular layer, and everything is moved at once so that it doesn't affect the layout.

- Linetype: an option that you can do with your piece, whether you want to cut a line, draw a line, or score a line.

- Mirrored image: reverses it, which is very important with transfer vinyl, so everything reads correctly.

- Print then Cut: it's an option that lets you print the design, and from there, the machine cuts it.

- Redo: does an action again and reverses it.

- Reverse Weeding: removes the vinyl that's left behind, and it's used mostly for stencil vinyl

- Score lines: helps you make creases in the papers so you can fold it.

- SVG: this is a scalable vector graphic that lets you cut a file that's scaled to be larger or smaller so that the resolution is kept, and made up of lines that consist of infinite white dots.

- Texts and fonts: let you use put specialized fonts and words within Design Space.

- Weeding: lets you remove the excess vinyl from designs. Press this when you're cutting vinyl.

- Welding: a tool you use when you want to combine two line shapes into one shape, and it's used to make seamless cursive words.

These are most of the functions you can do in Design Space. To use these, simply choose an image or font that you want to use and put it in Design Space. From there, you can do literally whatever you need to do with it – within reason, of course – and then put the image onto the material that you're using. For the purposes of learning, I suggest not getting in too deep with vinyl just yet and get used to using these tools. You also have pens, which can be implemented to help you write images with a tool that looks sharp and crisp. We'll go over the purpose of pens and what you can do with them in the next section.

Cricut Pens

Pens for your Cricut machine are essentially another way to get creative with your projects. I love to use them for cards, handmade tags for gifts, or even fancy invites and labels.

Now, each pen offers a little different finish and point size. They aren't toxic, and they are permanent once they're dried. You've got the extra-fine points for small lettering, up to a medium tip for making thicker lines. There are also glitter and metallic pens, so you have a lot of options to choose from!

But do you have to use them? Well, the answer is no. You can use different pens but test them on paper first and get adapters to use with them. Cricut pens are your best option. To use these, choose the wording or design, or whatever you want to do. You want to go to the layers panel that's on the right-hand side and choose the scissors icon – change that to the write icon. From there, you'll want to choose the pen color that you would like to use.

You can then have the design printed out on the material you're using.

Some people like to use different fonts, whether it be system fonts or Cricut fonts, or the Cricut Access fonts. However, the one thing with Design Space is that it will write what will normally be cut, so you'll get an outline of that font rather than just a solid stroke of writing. This can add to the design, however – you essentially change the machine from cut to write, and there you go.

You can also use the Cricut writing fonts, which you can choose by going to a blank canvas, and then choosing the text tool on the left-hand side, along with the wording you'd like for this to have.

Once you're in the font edit toolbar, you are given a font selection. You choose the writing font filter, so you have fonts that you can write with. From there, choose the font, and then switch from the scissors to the pen icon, and then select the pen color. That's all there is to it!

You can also use this with Cricut Access – if you're planning on using this a lot, it might be worth it.

To insert the pens into the Cricut machine, you want to choose to make it, and from there, you'll then go to the prepare mat screen. It will say draw instead of writing in the thumbnail this time around, so you press continue in the bottom right-hand corner, then put the pen into clamp A – you just unlock it and then put it in. Wait until it clicks, and that's it!

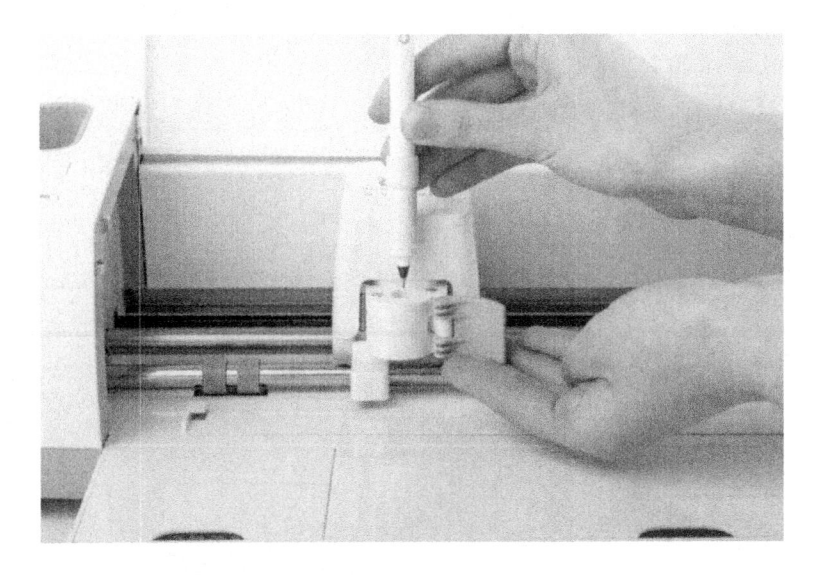

Cricut pens are super easy, and it's a great idea to consider trying these out.

As you can see, there are many different Cricut features and a lot of functions that may seem complex, but as you can see are really not that hard. There are tons of options for your Cricut projects, and a lot that you can get out of this machine.

Conclusion

In this book, we have given you the tools to make your Cricut work at its best all day, every day. When you can do this, you will be able to make anything that you want because these machines can cut amazingly well, and they have so many functions that it could make your head spin. If you have yet to purchase your first machine, I hope this helps your decision. We want you to enjoy Cricut Design Space, as much as the thousands of users all around the world.

Keep the tips and tricks provided close by as a reference guide, so you are not searching all over to find the answers to your questions.

Design Space makes Cricut a user-friendly, die-cutter, and I cannot stress enough how much you will get out of the machine as you learn each process. If you are a newbie, start slowly so you do not become overwhelmed, and abandon your machine without giving it a chance.

Frustration is common with first-time users, so read through this book carefully before starting your first project.

Using a Cricut machine should not be a new experience to you by now. However, it would be best if you kept an open mind to new updates. Cricut always give their users a lot of options to choose from, so, try as much as possible to carry out extensive research about their products, materials, and subscriptions.

Utilizing the tips and tricks in this book is not only going to help you to use your machine for any project that you want, but it will also help you make sure that your machine is in perfect working condition for as long as possible. Many tips and tricks that we have included in this book are things that most people would not have even thought of but are very simple, and they can help your machine last for a lot longer, than if you did not try them at all.

If you can utilize the tips in this book, you will be able to keep your machine in great condition, and make projects to your heart's content along with being more skilled. Once you can gain the skills you need, you will be able to go from simple projects, to professional projects, and you would be able to see in a store. Enjoy your passion and creativity and take it to the next level, while having a craft that is both innovative and fun. These machines are gaining popularity quickly because of all the things that they can work with. It is also a great way to make things for your children, or family members and can save you a lot of money in the long run when the holidays come. As such, this machine has even more options and benefits than you thought.

Cricut Design Space is entirely simple and easy to use, acing it doesn't occur without any forethought. That is for what reason I'm here to share my most loved Cricut Design Space instructional exercises, tips, and traps with you! These will change your Cricut life!

Printed in Great Britain
by Amazon